Awakening
A Personal Sojourn

Rick Joyner

MorningStar Publications
www.MorningStarMinistries.org

Awakening—A Personal Sojourn
By Rick Joyner

©2021 1st Printing

MorningStar Ministries, Fort Mill, SC. All rights reserved.

**Distributed by MorningStar Publications, Inc.,
a division of MorningStar Fellowship Church
375 Star Light Drive, Fort Mill, SC 29715**

**www.MorningStarMinistries.org
1-800-542-0278**

Unless otherwise indicated, Scripture quotations are taken from the New American Standard Version. Copyright © 1995 by Thomas Nelson, Inc. Used by permission. All rights reserved.

No part of this book may be reproduced or transmitted in any form or by any means, electronic, or mechanical, including photocopying, recording, or by any information storage and retrieval system, without written permission from the author.

Cover and layout design: Carlie McKinley

ISBN: 978-1-60708-676-5
For a free catalog of MorningStar Resources, please call 1-800-542-0278

TABLE OF CONTENTS

Chapter 1: The Journey Begins	5
A Broader World	7
Chapter 2: School	13
Dazed and Confused	15
Self vs. Formal Education	17
Chapter 3: Into Darkness	19
The Battles Begin	20
The Battle	22
Chapter 4: Saint Butch	29
Chapter 5: Hopes and Dreams	35
The Call	39
Chapter 6: An Anchor	45
Home Coming	49
Chapter 7: Gitmo	57
Decisions	61
Baseball Again	63
Chapter 8: Drugs and Demons	67
Chapter 9: Shipped Out	73
The Crisis	75
Chapter 10: Dropping Out	85

Chapter 11: New Horizons — 95
    Mary — 96
    First Vision — 100

Chapter 12: Reality — 103
    War of the Worlds — 104

Chapter 13: The Adventure Begins — 109
    To Fly Away or Stay — 112
    Revival Fire — 113
    The Devil Returns — 115

Chapter 14: A Peculiar People — 119
    My Favorite Miracle — 120
    Foundations — 122

Chapter 15: Like A Mighty Wind — 127
    A Consuming Fire — 130

Afterward — 135

Chapter 1
The Journey Begins

Don't be afraid of death so much as an inadequate life.
–*Bertolt Brecht*

The world was still staggering from the most devastating conflict in history, World War II. The Korean War was about to begin, and The Cold War, which would keep the whole world on the brink of annihilation for decades, was just starting to heat up. I was born anyway.

It was on September 7, 1949, at Rex Hospital in Raleigh, North Carolina. My parents were Harold and Janice Joyner. I had an older sister, Joanne, who was born four years before in Oakland, California. About six months after I was born the family moved from Raleigh to Richmond, Virginia. This is where I grew until I turned eighteen and entered the Navy. My brother Doug and sister Debbie were born in Richmond.

My first memories are of a happy family living in a small cottage. Two of my biggest addictions in life would begin while we lived in the first home I remembered. The first was when my dad gave me a ride on his motor scooter. I have been hooked on motorcycles ever since.

The next addiction came when we got Trigger, a beautiful female German Shepherd. Trigger had been an FBI dog, and she was given to us by my Uncle Bill, who was an FBI agent at the time. She immediately became my best friend. Thus began my love of dogs, and through them, animals in general.

That is all I remember about the first four years of my life—good things and good times. We then moved into a duplex in the Glenwood Farms neighborhood in Richmond. The next memory I have is walking in front of the duplex one day thinking how perfect my family was, and especially how my mother was right about everything. Every question I asked her at the time, she answered with seemingly otherworldly brilliance.

My mother was a brilliant person. I was told that she held the record for the most words typed per minute in the Civil Service during World War II. To this day I have never seen anyone type even close to as fast as she could, and with very few mistakes. She typed the manuscripts for my first books, which was a big help as I wrote them before personal computers and word processors had been developed.

My father was a loving, devoted, and affectionate man. It was a highlight of my day was when he came home from work. He and my mother seemed happy in those first years. I don't even remember an argument in our home during that time.

I looked up to my older sister, but don't remember her spending a lot of time with me. I remember overhearing conversations between her and my mother. She and Mom talked a lot, and I learned a lot from listening to those talks.

Everything seemed just about perfect in my earliest memories, except Trigger did not make the move with us to the duplex. I was never told what happened to Trigger, but I suspect that such a large dog would not have been allowed in those apartments. Even so, there were many other dogs in our neighborhood. There were no leash laws then, and I made friends with as many as I could.

One of my next memories is of the tall water tower behind our apartment bursting and flooding the field behind us. As we walked down to look at it I saw a German Shepherd on a chain that looked like Trigger. When I ran up to meet it, he bit me. Until then I don't know if I had even considered that a dog would actually hurt you, and I still remember the shock when he did. However, to this day I don't think I have been bitten by another dog. I am actually a dog magnet and I'm happy about it.

We must have gotten our first television just before the first station in Richmond began broadcasting. I remember sitting in front of it with the family waiting for the pattern to go away and the first program to start. Soon I was watching cowboy shows nearly every morning. My favorites were Roy Rogers, Gene Autry, and The Lone Ranger. I learned about good guys and bad guys and how to tell them apart.

In those times every television episode or story in a comic book had a clear moral message in it. Because of this our imaginations of becoming heroes revolved around doing something to save or help others. Good and bad were clear. Good people did what was good, but heroes were better than good—they risked themselves to help others. So, our dreams were about doing such heroic deeds that required great risk and saving people. Those who will be the greatest heroes in heaven still do.

A Broader World

I can't understand why people are frightened of new ideas. I'm frightened of the old ones. –*John Cage*

For the first four years of my life my family was my world. Then I began meeting other kids. There were about a half dozen boys about my age in the duplexes. We started playing cowboys and soldiers together, and refought just about every battle we saw on TV. In our world the good guys always won, and of course, we were the good guys.

One of the boys had an older brother who was about ten. We all looked up to him like our own big brother. He would tell us war stories and cowboy tales that he had read about that seemed even better than what we saw on TV. I think now that he may have embellished them some, but they were great. I couldn't wait to learn to read so I could read such stories. This would lead to another addiction of mine—books.

The first disappointment I remember is when I had saved my ten cent a week allowance until I had three dollars. It was like a fortune to me, and at that time it really was a lot of money for someone my age. When I proudly showed it to my father he said that I would be able to spend it when we went to the Washington Zoo on a family trip. Then he asked to borrow the money until he got his paycheck at the end of the week. At the end of the week he did not pay it back. He never paid it back. He probably just forgot it. Even so, until then I thought my parents were perfect, so this bothered me. It was not a big deal, but it was one.

The next jolt to my life that I remember came when a few of us kids were exploring a small patch of woods behind the duplexes. As we followed a path deeper into the woods we heard crying. Thinking they must be hurt, we ran to the sound. It was our hero big brother. He was being beat up by several guys about his age. It was a terrible shock to see him getting beat up like this, but seeing him cry was even worse.

We were so stunned we just stood there until the older boys started chasing us. Instead of running I tried to climb a small tree to get away from them, but I fell out of it and landed on a stump, hard. It knocked the wind out of me, and that was the first serious pain I remember. The older boys must have thought I was badly hurt because they left me to chase after the others.

The other boys had fled to a nearby backyard. I recovered and caught up to them just in time to see our big brother come walking out of the woods, still crying. To see him like this was really disturbing. He must have felt demoted in our eyes too because he did not spend any time with us again after that. What had been one of my favorite things, listening to our "big brother," was gone for good. It is sad how one negative event can so rob us of the good things in our life.

Until then I don't think I had even considered that you could know all about heroes but not be one, which is not totally accurate of course. Even great heroes may act cowardly at times, and the cowardly can be a hero at times. How we react in a moment of crisis can be determined by many things. Even so, studying heroic people and actions can help to give us the resolve to be courageous when we need to be. Pride can cause even the bravest to falter, and humility can allow even the most timid to rise above their fears and do brave things.

Of course, at such a young age I had not learned such truths, so I was more than disappointed in our older brother; I was disoriented. My father had taken my money and not paid it back as promised, and the one we looked up to as a hero turned out not to be one. This was how I began to learn the important lesson that no human being is perfect, and none can be perfect. Anyone can disappoint us at times, but that doesn't mean they will every time.

I now know that to keep trusting even after being disappointed is a key to the richest, happiest life. To become cynical is the path to darkness and depression. For this reason, it is better to resolve that we will not let our wounds, disappointments, or failures define us—but rather our successes. Failures are opportunities to learn, but successes are stepping stones.

At my age at this time, these jolts complicated things a bit, but life was still good. So, I guess I've always been an optimist of sorts. Everyone is struggling and probably trying to do the best they can. However, relationships are built on trust, and if we stop trusting people it can rob us of one of the greatest treasures in life—relationships. I didn't stop trusting people then, but became more cautious, which can also be wise.

The next big event I remember in my life was the birth of my younger brother, Doug. Everyone was really happy when Mom and Doug came home from the hospital, but it was a challenge for me. Since I had been the youngest until then I had been the main attention getter, and this was a definite demotion for me. That's a basic life lesson, but it was a lesson I didn't like. We're born self-centered and selfish, and one of the most important lessons to learn is how to make use of every lesson we can to get free of these two deadly thieves. Having a baby brother or sister can help.

But I didn't know that then. Being as selfish and self-centered as I was, I thought everything I liked was good, and everything I didn't like was bad. Maturing is learning that many of the things we don't like are the best things for us, like Popeye learning to eat his spinach. I was too young to get this message about Popeye though, and thought it just meant that we should always carry a can of spinach with us in case we got jumped by a Brutus. I asked Mom to buy some spinach after I saw this on Popeye, but hated it so much that I just thought I'd take my chances without it.

After Doug came I started learning to play alone more and enjoying it. This would be important for me the rest of my life.

I still need hours alone each day or I start feeling disconnected inside somehow. Later this would enable me to spend hours a day, and sometimes many days at a time, alone, reading, researching, writing, and most important of all, seeking to know God. I love being with people too, but I've always been a bit socially clumsy, and I feel this even more so when I have that disconnected feeling from not having enough alone time.

Not long after my brother Doug was born we moved to a new house in a new neighborhood a couple of blocks away. This was the first house that my parents had been able to buy. It was about a thousand square feet, with three tiny bedrooms, one and a half baths, a small kitchen, dining room, and a living room. To me it was a mansion. We had our own backyard, which Dad put a fence around for the new dog we were going to get. It didn't seem that things could get much better.

I don't think I ever saw my old buddies from the duplexes again after we moved. That was probably a good thing. After the disappointment with our "big brother" things had gone downhill pretty fast. Some of the boys had started doing cruel things to cats then dogs, and even puppies. I joined them once in this cruelty, and it left me with the worst feeling I had yet experienced.

How did we go from such high visions of growing up to be hero cowboys and soldiers, doing good for people, and then do such cruel things to helpless animals? The question is asked in Scripture: how can sweet and bitter water come out of the same well? I was disappointed in myself for a long time after this, and I think it was the first time I started to wonder if I might be a bad person instead of a good one.

Soon after we moved into the new house my sister Debbie was born. Since I had already been demoted by Doug's birth I was able to appreciate her more. Poor Doug only got to be the center of attention for about a year. I remember standing for long periods of time just watching Debbie in her crib. With the new house, baby brother, new baby sister, an older sister who was like a second mom at times, and our own backyard, I thought life was about as good as it could get. That was about to change more dramatically than I could have ever imagined.

Personally, I'm always ready to learn, although I do not always like being taught. *–Winston Churchill*

Chapter 2
School

The only thing that interferes with my learning is my education. *–Albert Einstein*

Soon after we moved into the new house school started. I was just starting first grade and this was a great adventure. My older sister, Joanne, had told me enough about school to make me really look forward to it. School was one thing that seemed to measure up to my expectations, at least through the first couple of years of elementary school.

One thing I had most looked forward to about school was to have books, and of course, be able to read them. When I learned to read for myself it exceeded my expectations. Reading became my door to other worlds and to great thoughts. I was addicted quickly, and I have never been cured!

A lot of kids lived on our block, and I got to know them much better as we walked the two blocks to school together every day. We talked to each other, which you could rarely do in the classrooms. We recounted television programs, funny experiences, and occasionally war stories heard from a parent, almost all of whom were veterans of World War II. Occasionally there would be a fight or scuffle, which added to the excitement.

Today, in some places, parents can be charged with child abuse for letting young kids walk to school alone like we did.

Of course, the world has become more dangerous, but this is a great loss. The first thing God said was not good is loneliness, and that walk to and from school each day was a big part of our social development.

My first-grade teacher is the only teacher I still remember well. I think this is because she was the only one devoted to getting to know each of us and for us to know her. Her name was Mrs. World. She was a large, elderly, and joyful lady. She tried to teach us to be good people; to develop our hearts and not just our minds. I did have other good teachers over the years, and I don't recall any bad ones, but Mrs. World stands out. She turned our first-grade class into a part of heaven that I could not wait to get to each day.

The first bad thing I remember at school was in the second grade. I was walking down the hall to my class one morning when I saw several girls standing in the hall crying. When I asked what was going on, I was told a boy in the next classroom had been shot. His father had been cleaning a gun and it went off and hit him in the stomach. He was not expected to live.

I had watched people get shot almost every day on television, but this was real, and it was a shock. I did not personally know the boy, but I felt terrible about it. The way the school reacted to this tragedy was remarkable though, and turned the whole experience into a positive life lesson.

We shared the grief, and we talked and prayed about it openly. Every class started the day with the Pledge of Allegiance, but beginning that day we prayed for this boy and his family right after this. When we learned that he would survive our prayers turned into thanksgiving to God.

When this boy returned to school some weeks later there was celebration. This terrible experience ended well. In fact, the kid got so much attention after this some of the guys said they wished they could get shot like he did. The main thing was we had all gone through it together, and when it was over we were even closer to each other. The bad had been used for good.

Dazed and Confused

Self-pity is easily the most destructive of the non-pharmaceutical narcotics: it is addictive, it gives momentary pleasure, and separates the victim from reality. *–John Gardner*

The next big memory I have of school was of Field Day. Next to Christmas this was the best day of the whole year. On Field Day the whole school spent the day outside playing games. There were races, and other field and track and competitions, as well as softball and kickball games. I was not fast enough to win any races, but I was fairly good at high jumping, and almost won a ribbon at that. When we weren't playing something, we would watch others compete, ate hotdogs for lunch, and there were drinks and other snacks available all day.

Then, when I was in the fourth grade there was a Field Day that would severely challenge my trust in teachers. One boy was so fast that he won every race he was in. In the last race of the day, he won, as we all expected. To the shock of the students who witnessed it, the teachers who were judging the race said that he had come in second, and gave the first-place ribbon to another boy.

The boy who had really won the race wept bitterly, and we were all upset. Several of us protested and were told to be quiet. Until this I was under the illusion that teachers were close to perfect, but what they did at that race was so wrong I began to distrust them all.

It's necessary to understand that no teacher, or anyone else, is perfect. Even so, what those teachers did in that race came across to us as blatant cheating and lying. This is what those teachers had been trying to teach us for years not to do. Some overheard the teachers trying to justify what they had done by saying this one boy had won all of the races, and it wouldn't hurt to let another win one. But the one they gave the ribbon to did not win! He knew it was wrong too, and seemed really embarrassed to be given the ribbon. This did not help him or anyone else.

This one thing was devastating to that little school. Until then it was like a piece of heaven, and we were all family, but this changed something in the very spirit of that school. It made a lot of kids cynical, and that is contagious. It may have been an over-reaction, but after this it was hard to trust anything the teachers said or did. That made it harder to learn from them.

This happened at about the same time problems started surfacing in my family. So, at the same time I lost trust in school and my family, which at the time was my whole world. It was like that German Shepherd I was so excited to meet suddenly biting me. It was totally unexpected. I went from trusting every dog, which is not smart of course, to looking at them all suspiciously until they earned my trust. Now it was that way with teachers and parents.

Disappointments are a part of life, and learning to handle them is an important part of our education. As I related, maybe it was because my life had been so great, even close to perfect up to this point, but some very disturbing things started to happen at home about this time, and it could have caused me to magnify everything. Once skepticism starts it will grow, and mine did from this point on.

Self vs. Formal Education

Good judgment comes from experience. Experience comes from bad judgment. *–Jim Horning*

Education is intended to prepare us for life, but it is also a major factor that sets the course of our life. From a young age I had a love of learning, and for the first few years I loved school. When this trust in my teachers was shaken, I made a subtle but firm departure in my heart away from formal education to pursue it in my way.

There were other factors in the course I took, but they would not have had the impact that they did on my education if it had not been for my loss of trust. So, I am mostly self-educated, which has positives and negatives.

Isaac Asimov said, *"Self-education is, I firmly believe, the only kind of education there is."* I am a strong believer in the merits of self-education, but this does not mean that there is no merit to formal education. I think the best education would include a proper balance of both. That "proper balance" would be different for each person and their goals or purpose.

Today the education system in America is in crisis and plummeting to the bottom in relation to other nations. It is failing because our education system has become more about indoctrination than education, as well as social engineering. The present system rewards mediocrity and conformity and punishes creativity and initiative in order to try to control predetermined outcomes. That is why most creative and successful people of our time have been mostly self-educated.

This is not meant to be an evaluation of education but to understand my story, my relationship to learning and education is necessary. My formal education was headed for disaster, but my education wasn't. I have been constantly told that I see things others can't. Some attribute this to a prophetic gift, which I do have, but much of the reason for this is not because of that. It is not because I am smarter, but because my mind works differently from those whose minds have been formed by the present education system.

Now those with more of a formal education sometimes see things I don't. That's why I think the best education includes both formal and self-education. All education should reward creativity and promote initiative, while establishing the necessary boundaries of effective systematic thinking.

You're not what you think you are, but what you think, you are. – *William James*

Chapter 3
Into Darkness

The mind is its own place and in itself, can make a Heaven of Hell, a Hell of Heaven. –*John Milton*

My first experience with the death of a loved one was not a person, but a chicken. I was in either the first or second grade when my parents gave me a live chick for Easter. I loved it from the first minute I saw it. I spent so much time with that chick each day that we bonded fast. In fact, I think it thought I was its mother or something, but it seemed to love me as much as I did it.

A lot of kids got these chicks each year, but it was rare for them to live long, and if they did they were given to farms. Mine lived and grew to be a very big rooster. He followed me everywhere, and I felt like he was my best friend. I would not allow him to be given to a farm, so we kept him as a pet.

My father and I built a little shelter for the rooster in the back yard, and he ruled our yard. I don't think a junkyard dog could have done any better protecting us. If anyone came close to our house without one of us being with them, he would fly at them in a most terrifying way. I don't remember him ever hurting anyone, but he may have come close to causing some heart attacks.

I think I loved that rooster as much as I had Trigger. However, he was not popular with our neighbors, especially since he woke them up every day at sunrise crowing. The first thing I did each day was go out to give him food and water and spend a little time with him. One morning I went out to do this, and he was dead.

I never saw Trigger dead, as she just kind of disappeared from my life. But there was my rooster laying on the ground, lifeless. He was the first pet I had to bury. To cover that rooster with dirt was the hardest thing I had yet done in my young life. It was not easy to get over, and for a long time I would visit his grave every day and sit there thinking about him being all alone under that dirt. I didn't know how to shake the loss. It was hard to think that I would never see him again.

We can't live long without learning about death. It is a part of our world now, and will be until the kingdom comes. One of the greatest of all promises is that when the King returns, He will do away with all sickness and death. Death is the last enemy to be destroyed, and it will be destroyed. But at this time I had no such hope, so I just hurt for a long time.

Then we got a puppy. It was another German Shepherd like Trigger, but a light brown male. I was sure that if he was not the smartest dog that ever lived he was at least in the top ten. I spent more time with Corky over the next ten years than with any other living being. He was not just a great companion, he was the most stable thing in my life during the times that would soon become so turbulent.

The Battles Begin

Adversity has nothing to do with determining your success—it is how we respond to it that counts. *(Unknown)*

If you had asked me before I was about eight years old, I would have likely told you that we were a wealthy family. It was at about that age I learned that we were not. We were lower middle class. Even so, we were happy, and life was good. I don't remember not having anything I really needed. Then suddenly it seemed that we had serious financial problems, and it seemed that many other insurmountable problems came cascading down upon us. The next few years would be a desperate battle to survive.

Those years of such struggle weren't without good times. Even so, there was a terrible darkness that was spreading over our family. It did not fight fair, and we did not know how to fight it. We just took shot after shot. I did not know of anyone else going through anything like we were, and that made it even harder.

When hard things hit your family, you can start to think you're being punished. When parents break up, the kids tend to blame themselves for it. When tragedies or crises come, we can become desperate for understanding, and not finding any, we often end up blaming ourselves or God. I didn't know God, but all that I'd heard about Him was really good, so I didn't blame Him. That made me start wondering what was wrong with us, or me.

That kind of thinking can lead to a black hole of self-centeredness that is almost impossible to escape. I would stay on the edge of that black hole for the next dozen years. I started to think that I was the cause of our family problems, and many years later I would find out that there was some truth to this. Since most of the emotions I was feeling at the time were not pleasant, I also learned to ignore my emotions.

Today I know that as deep as the wounds and hurts go into us, that's how deep the good and the true can ultimately fill us when we come to know The Savior. I've also learned that it is healthier to control your emotions than to cover them up. When I was this young I just did what I could to cover them up. The result was that I became insensitive. To this day I wonder if I would be able to feel some things more deeply if I had not so resolutely shut down my emotions when I was young. However, I was just a young kid and didn't know what else to do.

Until I was about eight years old, I could not imagine life being much better, then it quickly became unbearable and terribly confusing. There would be little reprieve for years. The ones I looked up to the most, my parents, were both overcome by a terrible insanity, so the main pillar of trust that my life was built on at the time was knocked completely out from under me. I would have trouble dealing with something like this now, but as an eight-year-old it was far beyond any possible comprehension.

Both of my parents were fighting powerful evil forces that they did not understand and so were defenseless against. They both got beaten down about as low as one could go. As I understand this now, and I am in awe of how they both kept getting back up to fight on as best they could. They both ultimately won their greatest battle and are now two of my biggest inspirations. Even so, as a young boy this struggle was a terrible and scary thing to behold.

The Battle

The supernatural is the natural not yet understood.
–Elbert Hubbard

I don't remember my mother ever being a really happy person, but she was pleasant until this time. She was cordial to our neighbors and people she met, but didn't have any close friends. Soon after we moved to our new house, she started saying negative things about our neighbors. Then she began to say terrible things about them. Even if those things were true, it is not the kind of thing you download to little children. I knew that they were not true, but I knew Mom really believed them.

Then she started saying terrible things about Dad's parents, Mother Dot and Daddy Pete. She then began almost endlessly berating my father from the moment he came in the door after work. We all begged her to stop, but she wouldn't, and kept getting worse. Ultimately it became an insane, seemingly non-stop rage.

Dad was working two jobs as well as serving in the Naval Reserve. He was doing this to try to make ends meet for the family, but I think he was also doing almost anything to stay away from home and my mother. Mom would start raging at him as soon as he walked in the door, and I think we rarely went to sleep at night without the background of hearing her insulting and berating him.

If Dad had to be home he would retreat to the little half-bath, lock the door, and would not come out until Mom was asleep. I didn't get to see him much, so I started asking him if I could come in and sit with him. We spent hours together on the floor of that tiny half-bath looking at magazines Dad would bring home and talking about them. We both loved airplanes, so we read and talked about them a lot. At other times we would look at pictures of boats or houses that we would like to own someday.

As strange as it seems now, at the time I really looked forward to those times with Dad squeezed into that little half-bath. What I hated more than anything was the several times each night Mom would bang on the door so violently that it scared the breath out of Dad and me. Then she would rage on for a long time at the door, so loud that Dad and I could not talk to each other. We learned to not say anything to her because if we did, or asked her to stop, she would just raise her voice even more, and the raging would last a lot longer.

As I think about this now I marvel at how patient my Dad was. He did react at times, but it was rare. Mom kept getting worse, and after a time it seemed she was standing at the door of that bathroom the whole night. Her raging was also getting more insane. I wanted to spend any time I could with Dad, but at one point I could not bear this anymore. Because there was really nowhere in the house to go to get away from it, I started sitting outside with the dog, or in the little shed we had if the weather was bad.

I started putting magazines and books in the shed to read each night. Even when it got cold I thought it was better in the shed than being in the house. I hoped Dad would come out to see me, but I don't think he ever did.

One good thing that came from this time was that my love for reading grew. Every night it seemed that I would learn incredible things, and my consciousness of the world grew. The bad thing was that this would be another factor that hurt me in school. What was taught in school was so boring compared to what I was learning on my own that it was hard to pay attention to it.

When I didn't think things could get any worse with Mom, I found out they could. While staying as angry and bitter, she added weird. One day she pointed out to me the way that the neighbors were hanging out their clothes to dry. As I looked she said that they were using them to signal each other about her. This was crazy, but it got worse. When our President had a meeting with the Soviet leader, she told me that they were plotting against her.

Everything in Mom's world was dark, sinister, and threatening. She tried hard to impose this view of the world on us. At times, she would make my little brother and sister and I sit in the hall in the middle of the house because she thought people were spying on us.

Dad finally had Mom committed. She was diagnosed as a paranoid schizophrenic, and one of the worst cases anyone had heard of. They gave her shock treatments. This had to be one of the most barbaric medical treatments ever devised, and it turned Mom into a seeming zombie.

Dad took us to see her at the hospital once and I begged not to have to do that again. I wasn't sure she even knew us, but the place was scary, the people were scary, and the condition Mom was in was scary. When she was released to come home she was a shell of herself. The shock treatments had wiped out all of her memories from the previous couple of years. So, our home went from being a place of unbearable strife and fear to another kind of really scary weird.

Even though Mom seemed disoriented, she was quiet. For a little while it seemed like we might be able to recover something of a normal family life again. That hope did not last long. First, she started being critical of Dad, then it got progressively worse until she was again spewing the same insane madness as before.

Mom was committed two more times, endured the shock treatments two more times, and came home each time even more like a zombie. Shock treatments cannot cast out demons. Drugs may be able to change behavior somewhat, but they cannot cast out demons either. In fact, drugs can be one of the biggest gateways to evil.

I started hoping that they would keep Mom at the hospital so that we could try to have something of a normal life at home. I had no understanding then of what she was fighting spiritually, so I went from not wanting to be around her, to not liking her, to hating the sight of her. At times I even wished that she would just die. She had turned our home into a terrible hell, and it was only bearable when she was not there. I felt terrible thinking this way, but it was how I felt. I was desperate for any kind of escape, any kind of peace and stability.

As soon as I was old enough I got a paper route. I had to get up hours before school to distribute the papers, and then go door to door to collect the subscription money at night. With school, this enabled me to be away from home most of the time.

Joanne was older and seemed to stay away most of the time too with her friends. I felt sorry for my little brother and sister who had to stay at home, but I hated to see my mother so much I only went home when I absolutely had to, which was late enough for her to be asleep.

When the weather was real bad Dad would get up and help me with the paper route by driving me in his car. I looked forward to these times to be with him. I could not understand what was happening with Mom, but I felt that all he had endured from my mother, and yet still tried to get help for her and be a father to us as much as he could, was amazing. Even though I did not see him much, Dad was an anchor, an island of sanity in a really insane world we lived in at the time.

Then one day I was leaving for school when Dad asked me to go for a walk with him. He had a very strange, euphoric look on his face that I had not seen before. As we walked he began to tell me that he was "the son of man" who had come to save the world.

I can't describe how distraught I was, if distraught is even strong enough to describe it. I don't think I ever contemplated suicide even in those times, but I do remember thinking it would be very hard to survive all that was coming at me at that time. This was too much, and I was pretty sure that my mind would snap soon too.

I had only been to church a couple of times until then, and I considered it a terrible punishment it was so boring. I did not know anything about The Lord except what I could remember from Dad reading us the Christmas story one time when I was four or five. I think he tried to talk to me about God a few other times, but I either did not listen or just could not understand. I had no clue who "the son of man" was, but I was sure Dad was in some kind of terrible delusion. It seemed that it was not even him talking to me, but he had become someone or something else.

I got angry. Then my anger turned to fear. Dad had been a rock, and now he was quicksand. I did not know of anyone else that had anything like this happening in their family. I could not get the picture out of my mind of the silly smile on Dad's face. I wanted to cry out for help, but did not know anyone I could turn to. There is no loneliness like when you feel an unseen evil cornering you, and you don't see any possible escape.

Soon Dad was committed. He was also diagnosed as a paranoid schizophrenic. He too was subjected to shock treatments. As bad as it had been with my mother, I had always loved and respected my father and wanted to be close to him. After that I wanted to get as far away from them both as I could. I lived for the day when I could leave all of this madness and strife and never look back. I would have left then if I'd had any idea where to go.

I had some good friends in the neighborhood, but for several years their parents would go from not wanting their kids to have anything to do with me, to taking me on trips with them and being really nice to me. I think they were weirded out by what was happening to our family, and would go from not wanting to get close to us and then feeling guilty and wanting to do something to help. Even so, I never knew when I went to visit a friend if their parents were going to run me off or be nice to me. Most of the time I got run off, so I started trying to avoid parents as much as I could.

I started to envy my friends' normal family life. I loved being at their homes when I could, and the feeling of a stable family was so wonderful I did not want to leave. Of course, this caused me to often overstay my welcome, and I would not be welcome back for a time. Then I would go back to the shed and read.

Life is a gift, life is happiness, every minute can be an eternity of happiness! *–Fyodor Dostoevsky* **(who wrote this just hours after nearly being executed by a firing squad)**

Chapter 4
Saint Butch

We will constantly be facing adversity. There will always be struggles to overcome... If you have a bad attitude, it is because you choose to have one. –*Dale Brown*

In the middle of the madness going on with my parents, a really bright light came into my life. It was a boy named Butch who moved in across the street. He was the most stable, sane person I knew at the time, and the nicest. He was kind, gentle, but strong in heart. It just seemed his nature to do good and be good.

Butch was three or four years older than me, but would spend a lot of time with us younger kids on the block. He taught us card games and board games. Then we'd sit for hours and talk about all kinds of interesting things that had an amazing way of inspiring us. I don't think I ever saw Butch angry, or ever say anything negative about anyone. He was just a good, kind, loving, and very interesting person.

I found out that Butch was a Christian when I saw him walking down the street one day and asked where he was going. He was going to a church about two miles away. My brief experiences with church were so boring I could not imagine any kid going to one if they were not being made to. When I questioned him about this, he agreed that some of it was boring, but he loved learning about God.

That was a stunning concept that we could learn about God, but if church was where we had to do this I couldn't understand why it was so boring. Even though I could not comprehend this at the time, it raised my respect for Butch even more. I wondered why his parents would not drive him there until I found out that they drank a lot and did not get up early on weekends.

Butch's parents fought a lot, too. One day I heard that Butch had been hurt trying to break up a fight between his parents. While he was in the hospital, they found out that he had leukemia and did not have long to live.

I was shattered, and did not know how to deal with it. Butch brought hope and goodness into my world. If there was anything worse than the craziness at home, losing the one bright light in my life at the time was the worst. Butch was my link to the stable, the sane, and the good. My hope for peace and stability was instantly turned into a crushing grief.

I tried to spend as much time as I could with Butch in the time he had left, but he got weaker fast. To my amazement he continued walking to church each Sunday for as long as he could make it. I would watch him have to stop and rest a couple of times just getting to the end of our block, but he continued to do this as long as he could. I didn't know God, and did not know how to pray, but I believed He was real. I could not help but wonder why He would let this happen to someone as good and faithful to Him as Butch.

Butch's funeral was the first I had been to. Seeing him lying in the casket was the worst thing I had experienced yet. I could not help but think about how he would be buried under the dirt like my rooster and be gone forever. There was talk about him being with the angels, and I tried to be happy for him about this, but I was too selfish to see anything good about that day. I hated that funeral service. I didn't know how to process what had happened to Butch. I had endured many bad days in my young life, but this one stands out as the worst ever.

When I got home from the funeral it was a bright, beautiful day that made me feel even worse as I thought about how much Butch would have enjoyed it. I could not handle the grief. There seemed to be no escape. Finally, I got on my bike and rode down the street as fast as I could, ending in the worst bicycle crash I ever had. I was not seriously injured, but painfully bruised and scratched up. The people who came to see if I was alright thought I was crying because of the pain, but I was crying for Butch. I could not hold it any longer, and it burst out like a flood.

My world was already hard, but Butch's death made it much harder. He was in terrible pain at the end, but he never complained. When I visited him the last time before he died, he wanted to talk about me and the other kids on the block. Actually, I don't remember him ever talking about himself. I could not understand why someone so good had to die.

Thirty years later a new friend, Mike Bickle, brought a man named Bob Jones to North Carolina to visit. When I walked up to Bob to introduce myself, he said he knew who I was. He looked me in the eye and began to tell me the reasons why the things had happened to my parents and to me as a child. In just a few minutes Bob made sense out of all of the twisted madness and confusion I had long before given up on understanding.

At the time I met Bob, I had been a Christian for nearly twenty years. I thought I had made peace with my past, but really I had just covered it up as something I would not likely understand in this life. When Bob spoke of what had happened to my family with such detail and insight, immediately a deep healing began. A terrible darkness began to lift off of me that I had no idea I was still under. Light casts out darkness, and the truth will set us free.

There was no doubt Bob's knowledge and insight into my life had come from God. Some of the things Bob knew I had not shared with anyone. Some I did not even know myself at the time, but they were confirmed during the next year. I knew in my mind that God knew and saw everything, but this transferred that knowledge from my mind to my heart. With this I knew that God not only knew, He cared and He had been with me through everything.

Bob was to become one of my best friends, and in some ways like both my father and Butch. He was the most kind, loving person I had met since Butch, and he would be a big part of my life for the next twenty-five years. With Bob I witnessed many miracles of physical healing, but many more that healed the souls and spirits of deeply wounded people like I had been. That kind of healing is more difficult than physical healing, and much of our physical illnesses are caused by what is in our soul and spirit.

You will read much more about Bob Jones in this story, but it will have to be a separate volume there is so much to tell. For now, if you think that you need someone like Bob to help you get over things in your past, pray for The Lord to send them. There are now many with gifts like Bob's, but you don't have to wait for a prophet to be healed. You have someone even greater who is with you right now.

Jesus is still doing everything He did when He walked the earth. He promised that He would be with us, and would never leave us or forsake us. We must not be like the cripple waiting for the angel to stir the waters so we can get healed when The King Himself is standing right next to us. Jesus is The Healer regardless of how or through whom He does it.

A great writer once said that suffering is a mystery, and we should respect it as a mystery and not try to figure it out. I disagree. The Apostle Peter wrote that the testing of our faith, or our trials, are more valuable than gold. The fruit they work in our life is eternal. Therefore, we must approach every trial, even every bad thing that happens to us, like finding a bag of gold. If we do not understand something it is because we have not yet reached the level of maturity and wisdom needed to, so we must use it to compel us to keep seeking Him who is the Wisdom of God.

Always remember, as deep as the devil is able to wound us, that is how deeply God can fill us. Do not waste your trials. Do not waste your afflictions—they were allowed to happen to you to call you higher.

Butch's death would have been devastating to me even if everything else in my life had been going great. As it came when I was already dealing with hardships beyond my ability to understand, I did feel for a time that I could not take any more, but then I would have to think of Butch. He went through something even worse than I did, but kept his incredible attitude to the end. His memory remained a rock of support that kept me going in the coming years. The witness of his faith and his courage right to the end gave me the courage and resolve to never give up.

Now I know for sure that Butch is not under the dirt, but is truly with The Lord and His angels. I can't wait to see him again.

**The function of man is to live, not to exist. I shall not waste my days trying to prolong them. I shall use my time.
–Jack London**

Military power wins battles, but spiritual power wins wars. *–General George C. Marshall*

Chapter 5
Hopes and Dreams

Honesty and frankness make you vulnerable. Be honest and frank anyway. –Kent M. Keith

As I related before, when my world at home was just starting to get crazy I became interested in sports. When I was six or seven Dad took me to work with him one time so we could listen to a World Series game on the radio together. This was before the games were broadcast on television. Listening to the games on the radio may have been more exciting because you had to visualize the game in your mind as you listened. That game sealed in my thinking that baseball was the greatest game, and The New York Yankees were the greatest team. Soon I had learned the name of every player on the team, their batting averages, and how many homeruns they each hit.

When I learned about Little League Baseball, I joined as soon as I was old enough, which I think then was eight for the "minor league" teams. I loved it more than anything I had ever done. The first game I played, I was put in right field. That's where you put the worst fielder because that's where the fewest balls get hit to. In my first game, a line drive was hit right at me, and I caught it. This astonished the coaches and probably everyone else. I was then moved to third base where you put one of your best fielders. I turned out to be good enough to keep the position.

When I was old enough to go to the Little League "major leagues" I started at third base. I liked the fast action you could get at third base, but I really wanted to be a catcher. The catcher was a part of every play and got to wear all of the cool equipment. One game we got far enough ahead that the coach gave in and let me catch. I fell in love with it, and was soon our full-time catcher. No one seemed to know then that this could give you "catcher's knees" that could hobble you for life, as I was to experience.

When we weren't practicing or playing Little League games, we would play pick-up games. If we didn't have enough people for a game, we would just play catch. We dreamed and talked constantly about being old enough to play in the big leagues, which we were all sure we were going to. We also started collecting and trading baseball cards, some of which I still have because my mother was smart enough not to throw them away.

Baseball was a good distraction from what was happening at home. I was good enough at baseball that it seemed to make me more acceptable to some of the parents of my friends, who were all big baseball fans. It's for this reason that I have such an appreciation for what sports can do for someone who has a troubled home life. I really don't know how I would have made it through this time without baseball. I know The Lord would have used something, but He did use baseball. It was my anchor of hope at the time that kept me from going insane.

One day my father told me that my grandfather, Daddy Pete, was coming to town to take me to a baseball game. We were going to see The Richmond Virginians, a Triple AAA Minor League team for The New York Yankees. The players may not have been Yankees yet, but they were future Yankees, and I had never been to any kind of professional game.

I was also a bit fearful about going to the game with my grandfather. He had never even talked to me before this, except for yelling at me a few times when I did something wrong when we were visiting. He was a big, tough, railroad conductor that had all of the grandkids pretty terrified. So I was excited about going to the game, but also really worried about spending time with Daddy Pete.

We had seats behind the first base line, so I got to see the future Yankees up close, hear the pop of balls being caught, and the smash of the bats. We even got to see a homerun. Daddy Pete only said one thing to me the whole night. About halfway through the game he leaned over and said, "Look how big and strong those men are."

I thought this was a message to me about how skinny I was, and how I needed to work out if I wanted to be a baseball player. Could he have come all the way to Richmond to take me to a game to tell me that? I thought so, and was encouraged by it. That meant he cared. But at that age I had no idea how to get bigger and stronger.

Later Daddy Pete gave me two of the most valuable gifts that have ever been given to me. They're two baseballs, one signed by the 1960 New York Yankees, and one signed by the 1960 Boston Red Sox. Daddy Pete was the conductor on The Silver Star, one of the modern passenger trains of the day. At that time the Major League teams rode trains between cities for their games. He had personally gotten those teams to sign balls for me when they were on his train. Some of the greatest players of all-time were on those two teams in 1960—guys like Mickey Mantle, Roger Maris, Yogi Berra, Whitey Ford on the Yankees, and Ted Williams on the Red Sox.

Going to that game with Daddy Pete helped baseball get an even deeper hook in me. I was getting better at it, and coaches talked to me about having a future in baseball, or at least getting a college scholarship. I couldn't think of a better future than playing baseball for a living, except for possibly flying the newest fighter jets.

Then one day I passed out while playing baseball in the back yard. It was a heatstroke. They can be caused by many things, but when it happened twice more it was obvious I had a problem with heat. After that I would get nauseous if it was a hot day and I had to be in the sun for more than a few minutes. It made matters worse that I was a catcher, which was the most physically demanding position, and you had to wear the extra equipment. Except for night games, I would feel nauseated the whole game, but learned to control it well enough to keep playing. Thankfully, most Little League games were at night.

My last year in Little League I made the All-Star Team. I thought I was having a lousy year because I had not hit a single homerun at the time they chose the All-Stars. Homeruns were how I measured how good a player was. So I thought I was having a bad year, but found out I had been chosen because I had the second highest batting average in the league. Even so, I hated anything less than a double, and tried to hit a homerun every time I got up. When I was told I had such a high batting average, I thought it was a revelation of how we can judge ourselves on one criterion like that and can feel like a failure when you're doing well.

I don't think any of the other kids on the block became a Little League All-Star, so this raised my esteem with them a little more. My parents' problems had devastated our family's finances, and my grades in school were tanking as it was almost impossible for me to concentrate in class. Baseball seemed a way for me to maybe get a scholarship, or even get drafted into the pros out of high school since my grades were so low it was not likely for me to get into college. But the problems I had with heat soon made it obvious I just could not play day games or even practice when it was hot, so a future for me in baseball was unlikely. This was a huge disappointment, and seemed to just be another blow to my life at the time. It turned out to be fortuitous.

The Call

Did you ever notice that people who like to do what they have to do always do it better? *(Unknown)*

One day when I was struggling with the thought of not being able to play baseball for a living, I had this sudden brilliant clarity that I was going to be a writer. This thought was so clear I believed it. I loved the thought of it. It actually gave me a lot of peace and vision. I don't think I told anyone else about how much I was reading, as I did not think that would go over well in our neighborhood. The thought of being a writer actually gave me an anchor of hope through the next years.

As interesting as TV was getting, I still preferred reading. As the problems in my family grew, my grades got worse. At times, I tried as hard as I knew how to turn them around, but could not keep the momentum going for long. It was just too hard to focus on the subjects at school because I had so much on my mind.

I was also sleep deprived from having to get up so early and stay up late for the paper route. Adding to that, by the time I was twelve, I was starting to stay out even later with some of the kids in the neighborhood.

I had my first sexual encounter when I was ten. The girl was several years older. It was about that time that I also got drunk for the first time. From that time on girls and partying added to my distractions.

I had little chance of passing 7th grade. I hated failing and watching many of my friends move on without me, but at the time school was the least of my problems. Teachers and others talked to me about how smart I was and how I should be getting better grades, but I had already determined that I would only endure school until I could legally drop out. I did enough to get by until I was expelled from school while in the 10th grade.

Even so, my self-education was going great. I had discovered *The World Book Encyclopedias* at the library. I had never found anything as interesting. The time I had for the library at school was limited, so I persuaded Dad to buy the family a set. At the time, it was a major sacrifice for him financially, but he did it.

Things were so bad at home I was often considering how I could run away, and that encyclopedia set may have kept me from actually trying it. I began with "A" and tried to read the entire set all the way through. To me this was like having my own gold mine to dig in every day. I was now addicted to knowledge like a junky, but allergic to formal education.

I was not good at sharing what I was learning though. I would sometimes awkwardly blurt out facts about something I had learned, but no one seemed interested. Every now and then I would share something with someone that would lead to a conversation, and this was satisfying, but rare. I longed for more of this type of interchange, and it seemed that school would have been a natural place for this, but it wasn't for the stuff I was learning was not taught in school.

Even in those days, school curriculum was dumbed down so that the slow would not be left behind. This also meant that the smartest and most diligent were bored and often the ones left behind because they weren't challenged.

I got a work permit and started working as a bag boy at our local grocery store when I was fifteen. By the time I was sixteen, I had saved enough for a down payment on my first car, a 1965 Pontiac GTO. Dad always loved cars and motorcycles, and so he cosigned for me to get the loan even though it was a stretch for me.

I also think Dad did this so that I would not be borrowing his car. I had wrecked one so badly it was "totaled" or could not be repaired. I had used it to drag race with some friends on a new section of Interstate 64 which had not yet been opened. Running off the end, the car had flipped three times in the air according to a friend following us. We were not wearing our seatbelts, and my only passenger, Steve Camp, was thrown out and landed on a railroad track. We were both taken to the hospital unconscious, but neither of us were seriously injured.

Angels? What other explanation could there be? With such a wreck, and for us to have just one broken wrist and some minor internal injuries between us, it was a miracle. I did not make the connection at the time that I was being divinely protected, but started feeling somewhat invulnerable. I was starting to hang out with a tough crowd, and drugs were coming into the picture. I "T-boned" a car while riding a motorcycle, and my body hit the car with such force it tore the top away from the main body of the car. I was basically unhurt except for a sore shoulder, so the delusion of being invulnerable increased.

I was still set on dropping out of school and was basically planning a life of crime when I ran into a life-saving distraction. Her name was Judy. She was a stunningly beautiful redhead, sweet, kind, and was the most genuinely humble girl I had met. She was way over my head, but she acted like she was lucky to have me. Without meeting her, my life was heading toward almost certain disaster. Instead of the crazy things I had been doing, I wanted to spend all of my spare time with Judy.

A couple of my close friends who were on the path I had been on died during that time while doing some of the crazy things I had been doing. About the only trouble I got in after meeting Judy was trying to sneak into the Richmond Motor Speedway to watch a NASCAR race. I climbed over the fence and came down right on a cop's shoulders. He laughed and graciously let me go, which kept alive the delusion I could get away with just about anything.

So as arrogant and lawless as I was, Judy helped stabilize my life. I am convinced that if it had not been for her, I likely would not have made it through those times without at least going to prison and maybe worse.

Another saving grace in my life at the time was the Peacher family. Bart Peacher had become one of my best friends. I met Bart and his older brother Jimmy I think while in the fifth grade. They lived on the same street but the next block over. Bart's family became almost a surrogate family for me.

Bart's mom and dad, Alice and Jimmy, were two of the greatest parents I could imagine. Compared to my family I thought they were one of the most stable families in the world. Actually, they were quite edgy too, but in a good way. Probably all families have some edge to them somewhere. This should be expected since families are made up of people, and when there were just two brothers on the whole earth they couldn't get along.

Mr. Peacher was a firm, but fair man. He always treated me with respect. He was also really funny. Bart's mom was more like Archie Bunker than Archie Bunker was (from the comedy *All in the Family*). Alice had opinions about everyone and everything, and she was absolutely sure she was right about every one of them. Her opinions never seemed mean-spirited, and were usually both outrageous and hilarious. People used to come from all over to listen to her. Hanging out at their house was like watching a sitcom, but better.

Two of my favorite memories of those times were watching Alice play penny ante poker, or watching Washington Redskins football games with her. You have never seen anyone get more irate over losing a nickel at poker, or go crazier over a Redskins fumble, than Alice would.

Years later Bart, Al Wood, and I were talking to the former Redskins coach, Joe Gibbs, and Bart told him how his mother had been buried in her Redskins paraphernalia (true). I told Coach Gibbs that it was only right that she was buried in it since it was being a Redskins fan that killed her! Alice actually lived a healthy life well into her 90s, but she may have lived past Moses if it had not been for all the stress she had during those games.

Bart also had a cute little sister, Bonnie, who I thought might be interesting when she got older. We did try to date a couple of times when I got out of the Navy, but something happened each time so it never worked out. We're still friends, and she's nearly as much fun as her mother was.

During our teenage years, the Vietnam War was ramping up. News began to filter into the schools about former students who had been killed in the war. It was not very clear what the war was about except to stop the communists, who were trying to take over the world. Even so, losing so many young people for a place no one had ever even heard of before was not going over well.

So, the turbulence in the world was increasing just as I found some stability in my life. There has been an anti-war movement with just about every war, but the one against Vietnam got traction, fast. Added to this, the Civil Rights Movement was exposing the many and terrible injustices and hypocrisies of the Jim Crow laws and segregation. It seemed that just about everyone under thirty started to dislike our own country, kind of like it is today.

On the fringes of these movements were smaller movements promoting everything from revolution to just dropping out of society altogether and join the counter-culture hippie movement. The whole world seemed to be going as crazy as my earlier life had been, so I gravitated toward what would give me more stability, not more confusion. I chose to do my duty and go in the service. It was a good decision.

Many people believe that cynicism requires courage. Actually, cynicism is the height of cowardice. It is innocence and open-heartedness that requires true courage—however often we are hurt as a result of it. –*Erica Jong*

Chapter 6
An Anchor

The only one who never makes a mistake is the one who never does anything. –*Theodore Roosevelt*

We had nuclear bomb drills when I was in elementary school. As we learned later, what they had us do in those drills would not have helped in a real nuclear attack. The real purpose of them seemed to be to teach us that the world was a really dangerous place and where the dangers were coming from—communism.

Of course, at such a young age we did not have a clue what communism was. As I grew and learned to study and check things out, it did not take long to confirm that this was actually true. The world is a very dangerous place, and Marxist-communists were, at that time, the most dangerous people in the world, especially to those who cared about freedom.

During these years, most were expecting World War III to break out at any time. It would obviously be a nuclear war. If that happened, it was likely that most, and possibly all, human life on earth would be wiped out. We grew up under this terrible threat of extinction.

With the probable imminent destruction of the human race coloring everything, it is interesting there were so many who set about to get educations, build careers, start families, and live normal lives anyway. I attribute this mostly to the extraordinary influence of what Tom Brokaw called "the greatest generation." Those who had endured The Great Depression when just finding enough to eat was a good day, to scaling the cliffs on D-Day in the face of Nazi machine guns and tanks, and subduing the fanatical Japanese war machine, had taught them to not only survive, but prevail. They had a mentality of forging on regardless of the odds. Some had been good at passing this on to their kids.

We had at least two serious war heroes living on our block. Many others may have been heroes as well because it seemed every father on the block had fought in the war, but hardly anyone talked about it much. Now they were trying to build a life, and they weren't going to let the commies stop them.

Even so, everyone knew how dangerous the emerging "Cold War" was. This tension would grow, and it was hard for all of the "baby boomers" to adjust to a world that could end at any minute. So many of them started thinking that since we were all probably doomed, why try to build anything? We should just drop out and party for as long as we can.

I knew some going in each of these directions. I was drawn to both in some ways, but having had such a chaotic childhood, I first took the route that would lead to more stability. Then I would try the other for a time. Both gave me an education about this world.

After the Cuban Missile Crisis many Americans started building bomb shelters. That brought up a third possibility—that there would be a nuclear holocaust but some could survive it. These would rebuild. This made it a patriotic thing to build a bomb shelter so that more Americans would survive than communists.

It may seem crazy now, but every political race was about who could better protect us from the communists that were trying

An Anchor

to take over the world. As people from school started getting killed in Vietnam, it became even more serious personally. At the time there were deferments for going to college or being married. I was not going to college, but Judy and I were getting serious, so marriage seemed a possibility.

Dad had inculcated into me a love of country when I was very young. It had been the histories of the Revolutionary and Civil Wars that I had first happened upon that gave me such a love for reading. As I read more of these, I was captivated about why so many were willing to risk their lives for freedoms that our country was founded on.

I had been especially inspired by how the tiny little colonies had arisen to take on the most powerful empire in the world in order to be free. As I read accounts of how people lived under communism, with the state basically owning them and not being able to make even the most basic decisions for themselves, such as where they wanted to live, go to school, or even work, I too thought resisting this tyranny was a worthy cause. I did not understand everything about the Vietnam War, but as it was a war against communism it was good versus evil.

Bart and another friend joined the Navy. When they came home on leave after boot camp I was intrigued with their stories. The Vietnam War was ramping up so fast that they started to do away with almost all deferments, so it looked like I was going to have to serve whether I got married or not. I went to see the Navy recruiter. To my dismay so many had tried to get into the Navy or Air Force that both of those services had stopped taking recruits. It looked like I would have no choice but to go into the Army or Marine Corp. Every day I went to the mailbox with trepidation, wondering if my draft notice had come.

The Navy recruiter had offered to let me take the entrance exam even though they could not take me as a recruit. I thought he had inferred that if anyone did exceptionally well on the test they might make an exception and take them. Because I had been such a terrible student I did not think I had much of a chance to do well on this test. I scored high enough on the test that they made an exception for me and took me into the Navy.

It was kind of like when I had made the All-Stars in Little League. I thought I was having a bad year, but had such a great batting average. All of my self-study had obviously taught me more than I had even considered.

To my further surprise, the Navy offered me a choice of vocations. Having had such a love of airplanes, I chose aviation and jet engine maintenance. After saying "no" to everything, they were now telling me "yes" to everything I asked for. I must have done really well on that test.

I was excited about going in. I would get to see some of the world I had been reading about. The other services could send you to a different country or two during your tour, but the Navy cruised all over the planet. Getting to work on airplanes was a bonus.

Selling my car was hard, but leaving Judy for long periods of time was going to be much harder. To get into the Navy I had to sign up for four years, and that was a long time to go with only seeing each other a couple of times a year when I had leave. I think we both knew it was over for us, but neither of us would admit it. When I left for boot camp we were still intent on getting married as soon as we could.

Me and two other recruits were given train tickets to Great Lakes Naval Base. One was a black man named Thomas. We were assigned to the same company at boot camp, and we became best friends. This, too, would bring some unexpected changes to my life.

Home Coming

All our previous positions are now exposed as absurd. But people don't draw the obvious conclusion: it must also mean that our present situation is absurd. –Terence McKenna

After boot camp we were given a week of leave before going to our next duty station. Thomas was going to the fleet, and I was going to Memphis Naval Air Station for jet engine school. Thomas had a one-night layover in Richmond, so I asked him to spend the night at our home. When I called to ask my parents' permission to bring Thomas home for a night, I didn't think to tell them that he was black. I had no idea it would be a problem. It was.

My parents were cordial to Thomas, but I could tell something was wrong. After Dad and I dropped him off at the bus station the next day, Dad let me have it for bringing a black man to our home. For all of the crazy things I'd seen in my parents growing up, I'd never seen racism in them.

This was a real shock. Dad even asked me why I didn't have white friends. I told him I had plenty of white friends, but Thomas became my best friend at boot camp. Then Dad lamented about what the neighbors must have thought seeing him come home with me. I was first shocked, then angry.

I don't remember any more of what I said to Dad, but I didn't want to stay at home for the rest of my leave. Thomas was a real prince, one of the best people I'd ever met. He was one of the most liked and respected men in our company at boot camp. He had as much character, maturity, and stability as anyone I had known. I counted myself very fortunate to have him as a friend, especially since at that time I was so lacking in character, maturity, and stability.

My parents' lack of appreciation for him just because he was black was more than troubling, but I had been naïve too. Virginia was very much a Southern state, and there were still many wounds and prejudices left over from the Civil War. The victors in every conflict get to write the history of it, but there are always at least two sides to a story. What I heard growing up in the South has rarely been told in the accepted accounts of the Civil War, but some have started to be researched and published recently.

America treated Germany and Japan far better after World War II than it had the South after the Civil War. What was done to the people of the South during the war, and for some time after it, would be a war crime today. I remember hearing some of these when I was young listening to my grandparents and great grandparents, who were telling firsthand accounts.

After the racism had surfaced so blatantly in my family when I asked my black Navy friend to stay overnight with us, it made me dig down a bit more into what was behind it. Most of the bitterness seemed to be about how so many Southern men had been killed in the war that there were not many left to defend the women and children from the waves of people who descended on them from the North after the war. Some former slaves were incited to join in to take advantage of the situation, and the raping and plundering of widows and others who were especially vulnerable became common, and continued for many years.

This led the surviving soldiers to band together to do what they could to protect the vulnerable and punish the "invaders." This led to organizations like the KKK emerging, which became perhaps the first major terrorist organization. Hitler even used the KKK and our "Jim Crow" laws as a pattern to use against the Jews in Germany.

The point is that Satan will not cast our Satan, and fighting evil with evil only multiplies the evil. So many deep wounds on all sides remain from the Civil War that have not been healed we now seem headed toward some even more trying times. How many families have buried their bitterness like mine obviously had? Was their hidden bitterness and racism open doors for the terrible insanity they later suffered? Is this not a cause of the insanity now surfacing in the whole country?

So, as a Southern white boy I grew up hearing one side of the story, and the young blacks would of course hear the other side. As is true of almost all accounts of history, there were truth and lies on both sides of major issues. But when you are deceived, you do not know you are deceived, or you would not be deceived.

My "woke" moment came with my parents' reaction to Thomas, and it caused me to investigate the merits of the Civil Rights Movement that was the foremost social movement of the time. Soon leaders like Martin Luther King, Jr., C.T. Vivian, and others became my teachers. I was astonished at how articulate and powerful their messages were and would listen to them over and over.

It seemed that the greatest orators in the nation were all in the black churches and the Civil Rights Movement. I learned that great oratorical gifts were highly esteemed in both. I was told that as great an orator as Martin Luther King, Jr. was, that in many black churches he would have been third string. From some I heard, I could believe it. I think if I had heard preaching like that in my previous experiences with church, I would have instantly been hooked instead of running off from boredom.

I was still in school when busing and forced integration came, and it seemed to really help my generation begin to appreciate the opportunity of getting to know those of other cultures. The first black kids sent to our school were great, and very quickly became some of the most popular students in the school. This was not just because they were black or different, but they were of extraordinary character and just great to be with.

Our parents had not had this experience. When I was young, I witnessed the Jim Crow laws that forbade blacks and whites to use the same bathrooms, restaurants, or even water fountains. This had to be more humiliating than any white person could probably imagine. I lament today how our education system indoctrinates more than educates, but some of the social indoctrination at this time was right, and to a large degree it worked.

I agree with Brokaw that my parents' generation may have been the greatest generation. To have struggled through all that they did to survive the Great Depression, and then to fight such ultimate evil as they did in World War II, and then the Cold War, they deserve to be honored. However, they were not great in everything, and they had not addressed the ultimate evil of racism.

What the Tuskegee Airman had done in World War II should have elevated them as some of the greatest American heroes of all-time. Instead, they had come home to be humiliated by the segregation laws and the incredible barrier to success and advancement that they were for minority families. This remains as one of our worst national disgraces. It also raises what the remarkable Tuskegee Airmen did even higher.

I am thankful to have grown up when some of these profound issues would determine whether America would truly be a place of "liberty and justice for all," or just for some. At times I would become cynical, but mostly I was thankful to live in a country that had been willing to fight a Civil War to end slavery, and persisted with the Civil Rights Movement until there was progress. Even so, we obviously still have much to do

An Anchor

to rid ourselves of racism. What better country in the world to face these issues than one that is made up from probably every other nation and culture in the world?

In the Navy, it seemed that racial discrimination issues had already been settled for the most part. The official policy of the Navy was to judge everyone on merit and ability, and it seemed to generally be the case. But the country we were serving was having a huge struggle with this. I had only been away for a few months for boot camp, but it was shocking how my family and almost everything about Richmond had changed. Most of my friends had either gone into the service or to college, but even those who were left seemed really different now. Of course, they had not changed that much, but I had.

I spent most of my time on that first leave with Judy. We had a great time, and were trying to figure any way to keep our relationship going, but just before I had to return to duty, we faced reality and broke up for good. I was changing fast, and I did not even know if I would come back to Richmond again I felt so disconnected to it.

My next duty station was Naval Air Station Memphis. I felt more at home on a Navy base than I had in Richmond. My life had been so chaotic that the routine of military life seemed to give me needed order, security, and peace. In the Navy you knew your place and what was expected of you every day. The schools were practical, interesting, and challenging.

When you went to a new assignment or duty station you rarely knew anyone else, so it was easy to become close friends in just a few days in the military. I was ultimately sent to a number of different schools and duty stations, so I was repeatedly put in situations where I did not know anyone. I seemed to meet great and interesting people at each one, and started enjoying going to new and unknown places.

Marines and sailors were in these tech schools together since the Marine Corp is a part of the Navy. Interestingly, there was a bigger division between Marines and sailors than between the races. Even so, as it turned out the best friends I made while at these schools were often Marines. I'm still not sure why. Marines tended to be far more serious about the military and its discipline than sailors, and I was probably one of the least serious of the sailors. Even so, somehow I often ended up with my best buddies being Marines.

While stationed in Memphis, the first anniversary of Martin Luther King, Jr.'s assassination came. He had been killed in Memphis, and they were expecting riots to break out in town, so we were restricted to the base. Rumors circulated that some of the blacks on base were planning to riot. It was a lie, and an evil one. It was the first and only racial discord I remember while in the Navy. In a place where there seemed to be little or no racism, suddenly every black was a suspect, and the black sailors felt threatened by the whites. This was bad for whites, but I can't imagine how the black sailors felt.

I wanted to understand the issues better and so I tried to talk to blacks in the school about it. Most did not want to talk to me, but the few who did gave me quite an education. What they had suffered, and yet were still in the military willing to serve their country, was inspirational.

In all of my reading and study, major social issues had not been much of a draw to me. I was not a "change the world" type then, but mostly trying to find some peace and understanding from the troubles in my own life. Getting to know some great people who had been treated so unjustly, but remained of such high character, helped get my attention off of myself and more on what was going on in the world.

After graduating from the Memphis jet engine school, I was sent to the Naval Air Station in Jacksonville, Florida. This was to attend an advanced school on the F-8 Crusader fighter aircraft that was flown by the squadron I was being assigned to in Guantanamo Bay, Cuba. Though this was an advanced course, I had become so interested in jet engines that I was studying them on my own. So, this was an easy course for me, which meant I didn't have to study much. This gave me time to become an expert on liberty, which is what off-duty time is called in the military. This allowed me to find Flagler College in St. Augustine, Florida, an all-girls school at the time.

The girls at Flagler came from some of the wealthiest families in the country, and were not only cultured, they all seemed to be beauty queens. Once I discovered Flagler, it consumed all of my off-duty time.

Then the dreadful day came when I graduated from school and had to leave that single man's paradise for Guantanamo Bay, Cuba. The base there was so isolated that there were probably not a dozen single girls out of high school on the entire base. This was a serious shock after the time at Flagler, but a needed one.

The flight to Gitmo on the World War II vintage cargo plane was unbearably long, more than twelve very uncomfortable hours. We were going so slow I kept looking out the windows to see if ships were passing us. But this gave me some good time to plan. So, I decided not to waste time seeking out the few potentially available girls on the base, but to spend my free time there reading and studying. It was a good plan.

We need to take dreams more literally, and waking life more symbolically. –*Robert Moss*

If you do not know where you're going you'll end up somewhere else. *–Yogi Berra*

Chapter 7
Gitmo

Don't count the days; make the days count. –*Muhammad Ali*

Gitmo is what Guantanamo Naval Base is called. Located on the southeastern part of the island of Cuba, it was a huge but isolated base surrounded by the hostile forces of Fidel Castro. This base was considered one of the two worst duty stations in the Navy at the time, with the other being the South Pole. Contrary to the quote, "Don't count the days…" noted above, you could ask any sailor at Gitmo and they would know exactly how many days they had left in their one-year stint at the base.

Our squadron, VC-10 was at the Naval Air Station across the bay from the rest of the base. This made us even more isolated. It was barren, literally a dessert. I loved nature and animals, but this place had no beauty, and the main creatures were reptiles like Iguanas (lizards 3-4 feet in length), boa constrictor snakes, and tarantula spiders nearly as big as your hand. What made it even worse was that a number of guys in the barracks had made some of each of these terrors as pets, and they would sometimes get loose in the barracks.

So my new duty station was even worse than I had been told. Even so, I was determined not to waste a whole year of my life, but was going to enjoy it and benefit from it. The starkness of the place just meant I would have even less distractions from my studying.

Having landed just before midnight of Christmas Eve, for Christmas I decided to go to the roof of the barracks and get a little sun. It was hot, so I stayed up there for less than a half hour, but got so sunburned I almost got court-martialed. In the military, if you did something stupid to hurt yourself it was considered "damaging government property" (not kidding).

It was a very painful beginning to this expected terrible tour of duty at Gitmo. Since it could hardly get any worse, I thought it must get better, and it did. The year at Gitmo turned out to be a really good time, almost like a vacation.

I read many books, and I learned to dive. The waters were some of the best in the world for diving. I went diving almost every day with a couple guys from the squadron. We did a lot of spearfishing, but I enjoyed just swimming around looking at the different creatures, coral, and the very colorful underwater beauty that was the opposite of the barrenness of the land above.

The club was walking distance from the barracks. It was a beautiful outdoor facility on a cliff overlooking the Caribbean Sea. A beer was ten cents, and mixed drinks were a quarter. I spent many enjoyable evenings there watching thunderstorms form out at sea, which gave an almost nightly fireworks show. One night the storms grew larger and faster than I had seen before. They started bunching together, and there was a number of waterspouts. It was quite a show. Later we were told that we had witnessed the beginning of Hurricane Camille, one of the deadliest to ever hit the U.S. Gulf Coast. I was fascinated by it, and this began a desire to understand weather and climates.

Because we were surrounded by hostile forces, everyone had to go through basic infantry training with the Marines in order to be a part of the ground defense force. After that training, working on the flight line, and then in the jet engine shop, scuba diving, playing baseball, going to the club, or to a movie shown at our big outdoor theater were about the only things to do there. Except read. I did all of them, a lot.

So, I was well enough entertained. Being in the squadron was better than being on the base crew, or the Marines. We could fly the squadron S-2's (anti-submarine warfare planes) to the different islands, and occasionally back to Florida, for liberty. We could also catch rides to the other islands on ships passing through the area that would sometimes dock at the main base. Our skipper almost always let us take time off to do this since we were deprived of the usual liberty available to other bases. Over the year I got to know a number of the islands pretty well.

After doing a short stint as a plane captain on the flight line, I was promoted to petty officer and assigned to the jet engine shop. I loved working on jet engines. We had a great Chief who would teach us as much as we wanted to know. I spent most of my duty time learning more about the engines and other systems on the aircraft, which was fascinating.

As a teenager I had learned to do minor repairs on my car, and found there is a special satisfaction in being able to track down the cause of a problem, and then fix it. Mechanics have an especially rewarding job, but working on jet fighters was next level. So, I really enjoyed going to work each day.

Our Chief was an educated man in many fields, and his interests were similar to mine. He gave me some good books to read, and when work was slow we spent hours talking about things I don't think either of us had ever had anyone to talk about with before. He was the first one I remember having any seriously in-depth political discussions with.

There was a great nightclub on main side called The Copa Cabana that he invited me to so I could meet his wife. A few of us started going to it quite often for the music and great food. Since there were hardly any single girls there, we mostly just sat and talked. The Chief was working on a PhD, and sometimes we discussed his courses. I think these talks with the Chief taught me a lot about how to discuss serious matters with serious people. It is a skill few people have, and it is necessary if you're going to move in circles with high-impact people.

After just a couple of months in the shop I was picked to lead the night crew for the jet engine shop. In this position I was in charge of everything in relation to the engines, including inspections, repairs, removing and replacing them in the planes when needed, running them and "trimming" them to adjust for maximum efficiency, and then signing off of them to be put back on the flight line. That was a lot of responsibility for a nineteen-year-old, but I did know what I was doing because I had been trained so well. No one seemed to think it was a big deal to have someone nineteen over the night jet engine shop.

The military is very good at getting to know each person, finding out what they will be good at, teaching them, training them to do it well, and then giving them as much authority and responsibility as they can handle as soon as possible. This may be why so many who become leaders in virtually every field are those with military experience. They teach leadership to everyone at any rank and any job.

Since the Navy I have built and run two fairly large organizations, and I've gotten to know top leaders in many fields. The military may have some issues with efficiency in some areas, but overall, every organization I have ever gotten to know could benefit greatly from some basic military management systems—the government itself being the most in need of this. For this reason, I counsel many young people who have leadership potential to consider doing a stint in the military. This could help virtually everyone, and for some it will multiply their potential for success at whatever they do.

Decisions

It is never too late to be what you might have been.
–George Eliot

Even though it was enjoyable to work on jets, I still dreamed of flying them. One day our division officer asked me to meet with him. He said that I had scored so high on all the tests I'd been given by the Navy that they wanted to send me to engineering school, and then Navy Flight School to become a pilot. One of my ultimate dreams had been to be a fighter pilot, but with the wreck my formal education had been I had thought it was impossible. The Navy did not, even though they knew my school records.

Now think about this for a minute. An organization as large, serious, and as steeped in tradition, with such a high devotion to excellence, having the flexibility to see potential in someone like me. They laid out a path for me to become an officer and potentially high-level leadership. We may not think of the military this way, but they are a people business, and they are devoted to knowing and developing their people to their highest potential, drawing the best out of their people, and they are very good at it.

I talked with my division officer about this for a couple of hours. We both asked a lot of questions. I told him about my dream of flying fighters. Being a fighter pilot himself, he assured me that it was even better than he had dreamed. But then he said that it would not be determined what kind of plane I would fly until I graduated from flight school, as that had to be determined by what the Navy needed at the time.

I told him that I would consider it, but I ultimately declined the offer. With engineering school, flight school, and then being obliged to six years of duty, it would almost certainly mean a commitment to making the Navy a career. I would have done it if they had guaranteed me fighters.

If I carry any remorse about major decisions I made in my life, this might be one of them. It was also the first of a pattern of really attractive offers I received that would have sidetracked me from my calling. At this time, I did not know I had a calling, but I had a sense of purpose to be a writer. I had come to really like the idea of a life of study and research, which was a chief joy that I had.

So, I planned to use my G.I. benefits when I got out of the Navy to go to journalism school. It's hard to say how things would have worked out for me had I chosen the Navy offer, but I do think it would have caused me to miss much of what I was called to do in ministry, which is even better than flying fighters, since I have now experienced a little of that too.

Several more times in my life I would have to choose between my calling and a tempting opportunity. Of all that I have talked to about this who are walking in a high-impact ministry, I have not met any that did not have to resist tempting offers to stay on course. As I had these offers come to me several times at the beginning of a major new demarcation, only once did I wrongly choose the opportunity, and it cost me ten valuable years. I'll have more to say about this later.

The Navy had given me a lot already with the schools and on-the-job training. They gave me responsibility and stability. The discipline was severe if you messed up, but it seemed that the nature of the Navy to promote everyone as much as they could. I did not appreciate it as much then as I should have, but now I am very thankful for the experience. In fact, I consider it a basis of what I have been able to accomplish since.

Baseball Again

If at first you do not succeed, you are like most people. (Unknown)

Cuba was the hottest place I had ever been. Working days on the flight line was hard with my sensitivity to heat, so being promoted so quickly from the flight line to the air-conditioned jet shop might have saved me from another heatstroke. When I found out that the squadron baseball team played only night games, and most of the practices were also at night, I joined the team.

We had a pretty good team, but having to catch the ferry over to the main base to play our games sank us. The team drank far too much beer on the crossing. Many of the players we faced were Major League players in the Naval Reserve to avoid Vietnam. They had made deals with the Navy so they could come to Gitmo to play in the winter to keep their skills sharp, and at the same time complete their military obligation. We did not win a single game that year, but we were the most popular team. For some reason every team wanted to play us.

There have always been few catchers that were also good hitters, even in the Major Leagues. I was a good catcher, and I had one of the top batting averages in every league I played in. I was told by some of the pros in the Gitmo league that I had the skills to play in the big leagues, both catching and hitting. Playing against so many good players gave me the confidence that I could, but I didn't know how I could work around the heat problem.

I could have gone to the doctor to see if there was any kind of medication or therapy that would help and allow me to play ball in the day time, but I had hidden this issue from the Navy and thought I could cause a problem by bringing it up. This was possibly another big missed opportunity, but I now look at it as another potential diversion that would have steered me away from my calling. I did later go on to fly planes, but I never did play organized baseball again after Gitmo.

Now, having lived seventy plus years, I have watched many people choose opportunity over their calling. I've come to believe that in this life most people miss their true purpose because they follow temporal opportunities rather than seeking the kingdom first.

I've also witnessed people that have missed their calling a number of times, but The Lord keeps giving them more chances. When they finally make the right choice The Lord helps them make up for lost time. We serve a very gracious God.

I think I have only missed making the right choice once, but I could have missed many more times than I realize. I also don't think any but One, Jesus, has been perfectly obedient and always made the right choice. It would not shock me on Judgment Day to find out I had really missed in major life choices many more times than I got it right. This is something I've become far more sensitive to because the one time I know I missed was so costly, and I've witnessed many others making very bad choices over the years that were also costly.

Many sports are a mirror on life. I don't want to dig down too deep on how this is true with baseball, but in baseball even the best hitters fail two-thirds of the time. The best hitters of all time failed more than 60% of the time. I wonder what "batting averages" most people would have in life for hitting the opportunities that come their way.

Good hitters in baseball learn to let the pitches pass until they get "their pitch," the one they can do the most with. We must let some pitches that come our way pass as well. If we look back on our lives as so many opportunities missed, we're probably just like everyone else. However, one right choice seems to be able to make up for many misses. Who remembers the strike outs a player had in a game if he gets the game winning hit? We will be used by God if we just stay in the game and don't quit.

Try again. Fail again. Fail better. –*Samuel Beckett*

You may insist on all or nothing and achieve nothing.
–R. Redwine

Chapter 8
Drugs and Demons

Learn from the mistakes of others. You can't live long enough to make them all yourself. –*Eleanor Roosevelt*

Since we could not go off the base into Cuba because of Castro, for off-base liberty we had to fly squadron planes to one of the islands in the Caribbean, or back to Florida. This is when I discovered Jamaica and Jamaican marijuana. At the time it was considered some of the best in the world, so I soon started going there regularly.

This was the late 1960s and the counter-culture movement was growing around the world as well as in the U.S. Almost everyone was getting turned onto pot, including a high percentage of those in the military. There was actually a pretty big drug underground in the military. Those who were in it could spot others who were by subtle signs. There were secret places to smoke, but you had to be in the club to learn about them, and the vetting was strict because everyone was afraid of being busted.

Most who were smoking pot or doing drugs in the military tried to be responsible enough to not get too stoned when in intense or highly challenging situations, such as combat or flying airplanes. Some learned how to be stoned and keep functioning at a pretty high level even in highly technical jobs. No doubt it had to affect our readiness and performance to some degree, but we all thought it made us better at everything we did. In fact, we thought it made us geniuses. You think like that when you're stoned.

Very few that I knew in the Navy got into anything harder than pot, except for a few who did psychedelic drugs like mescaline or LSD. I liked the psychedelics, but was resolved to never do anything seriously addictive, and I never did. I enjoyed partying and having a good time, but I also still loved to think and read, and I wanted to understand what I was reading. I never liked getting drunk or too stoned. I was known as a "mellow head," but I stayed that way pretty much all the time.

I witnessed some people get really weird on drugs, even as weird as my parents had been. This caused me to wonder if there was some relation to drugs to what had happened to them. I knew they weren't doing recreational drugs, but wondered if they had reactions to medications or prescription drugs psychiatrists had given to them. Later I found the connection, and the insight began at Gitmo.

One night the Chief told me about finding accounts of very strange events and sightings of things like UFOs in our part of the Caribbean. Some claimed to see birds as big as airplanes. Because most of our training flights were in or close to the Bermuda Triangle, things like this got our attention. There were sometimes bizarre things that happened on these flights no one could explain. Then one night, as a few of us were on the roof of the barracks smoking pot, we all saw the big birds, and they were at least as big as a large plane.

Hallucinations? I'm confident they were. We checked later to see if anything like this had been picked up on radar by the base, but they had not. We all saw them at the same time, and described them the same. Were the islanders doing the weed hundreds of years ago when these sightings started? Perhaps.

Even though I knew these were likely hallucinations, I also felt something supernatural about them, and it did not feel good.

Then one of our squadron planes had a most disconcerting experience on a flight. The plane was met by security when it landed, including the base commander. The entire crew was put under a gag order not to tell anyone what happened. That spooked everyone, but especially those on flight crews. We resolved to find out what had happened.

We finally got one of the crew to tell us in exchange for a bag of Jamaican. The plane had lost all communications, even though it had two backup systems on board. Then it lost the navigation systems, and ultimately they lost control of the plane. The plane seemed to be steering itself. For most of the flight they had no idea where they were, and felt that they were in some kind of twilight zone. Before running out of fuel they regained control over a friendly island where they were able to land. Repair crews were sent to fix their communications and navigation gear, and to escort the plane back to base.

When I talked about this with the Chief he said something very curious. He said he thought these sightings, and strange events like this plane experienced, were connected to the strong black magic and voodoo in the region. A few years later I was to learn that this was indeed the case.

As I have been working on this book the U.S. military has started to open its files on UFOs. Since our experiences, I have become convinced that UFOs and other such phenomena are sightings of supernatural beings like those described in The Bible, not visitors from other planets. This is becoming much more of an interest now because the supernatural incursions from both sides, good and evil, are increasing in these times. I think these are both angelic and demonic activity.

I have reasons for this but do not want to get too into this here, but since these things are in the news almost daily now I wanted to mention it. If you'll do the research you'll find that these sightings increase dramatically when there are threats or conflicts in the Middle East, as many biblical prophecies are now unfolding there.

The affect these experiences had on me was to steer more of my thinking and research to religions, philosophy, and the history of the region. The whole area seemed filled with supernatural activity, but at the time I didn't really believe in the supernatural. I didn't disbelieve in it either, I just didn't know. I did feel that what was happening was very weird, and it had a really bad, sinister feeling to it.

This was a period in my life when I was gaining a lot of knowledge about a lot of different things. As related before, it was not as disciplined and sequential as formal courses would have been. In some ways this may have been better. I was studying what I wanted to know, and what I was experiencing, not what I needed to study to pass a course. I cared about what I learned, and this seemed to help me see insights that others in more systematic courses seemed to miss.

When I was able to discuss some of these subjects with people that had a formal education in them, I was able to hold my ground. This was encouraging to me, but also fed my arrogance. I started deceiving myself into thinking I was in pursuit of some ultimate truth and understanding, including what had happened to my parents, my childhood, and myself. I was still confused and troubled, and at times desperate for some great mooring for my soul. In all of the places I was looking for understanding, I never considered Christ.

That may have been a good thing too at the time. I was often remorseful that I had not grown up in a strong Christian home and come to know The Lord early, but for me, I think it was His purpose that I had some experiences first. After scouring the depth of those considered the great teachers in so many other faiths and disciplines, and seeing how shallow and often contradictory they were, I was able to appreciate Christ and the true teachings of Christianity far more than I would have otherwise.

I don't remember a time in my life when I would not have liked to know if God existed, at least on the few occasions when I thought about it. I did consider, and sometimes said, that if I found God it would be the utmost foolishness and waste to expend my life on anything less than seeking to know Him, and if possible, serve Him. I meant it as much as I could.

The one thing I may have had that would have enabled me to see God as He was, and not just what I wanted Him to be, was the subtle desperation for the peace I thought would come with understanding the world. It did not. My peace would not come from this world, and I now think that is the last place anyone will find peace. As I grew in knowledge of the world I became more disturbed by it. This was all leading to an awakening.

I was also to learn just how much drugs can be demonic inroads into our life, the gates of hell through which hell gets access to us. The temporary pleasures they can bring can also lead to long-lasting devastation.

Since the initial publication of the chart of the electromagnetic spectrum, humans have learned that what they can touch, smell, see, and hear is less than one-millionth of reality. –*R. Buckminster Fuller*

It is better to do the wrong thing than to do nothing. – *Winston Churchill*

Chapter 9
Shipped Out

Life is something that happens to you while you're making other plans. –Allen Saunders

After Gitmo I was assigned to yet another school on the A-6 Intruder attack aircraft. This was in preparation for going to VA-34, a squadron stationed on the newest aircraft carrier at the time, The USS John F. Kennedy. The ship was based in Norfolk, Virginia, but our squadron was based at Oceana Naval Air Station in Virginia Beach.

Bart Peacher and I had kept in touch, and his ship, The USS Independence, was stationed at Norfolk too. When we found out that our ships would be in port at basically the same time, we decided to get an apartment together in Virginia Beach.

They say if you remember the 60s you didn't really experience them. That must be what happened to the next year for me. What I do remember was pretty much a constant party every night with the local hippie crowd and beach bums.

When in the military, if you are not in combat you are training to be. War is such a serious business that it was top priority for everyone to constantly be getting better at what they did. Even so, when we were in port, the Navy tried to give everyone as much free time as possible because at sea there was no liberty, and we often worked eighteen hours a day. The Navy also gave us a nice allowance for living off base if we chose to. I thought this was about as perfect a life as I could have planned at the time.

It ended up with a huge bust, and many of our friends going to prison for drug possession and distribution. Bart and I did not get caught in the bust, but Bart went AWOL and was caught after a few weeks in Wichita. To make my own subtle protest to the Navy for participating in that bust, I made the beneficiary of my military life insurance the War Resisters League. This got my security clearance jerked, I was no longer allowed to work on the planes, and I was restricted to base until the ship sailed.

For some reason I did not get busted in rank. Because I was ranked too high to be given menial tasks like cleaning or painting, I was assigned to the squadron ready room where the mission briefings took place. I assisted in preparing these, which seemed a bit weird since I did not have a clearance, but I was not going to complain as I may have had the cushiest job in the Navy. I had very little to do, and so I read, or played chess with the pilots and crewmen, all day every day.

I don't think I lost a chess game for the rest of the time I was in the Navy and was called the ship's chess champion. This meant that I was constantly challenged. Through this I got to know many of the pilots and other officers and crew from the ship. Some became friends.

Our squadron Commander would sometimes take me to his stateroom and talk to me about politics. He was trying to convert me to becoming a conservative, or at least more of a patriot. I appreciated him caring enough to make the effort, but I was pretty incorrigible at the time. Later, when in the Mediterranean and I got into trouble in Greece, he saved me from some very bad consequences which I'll share later.

The Crisis

> Life is made up of a series of judgments on insufficient data, and if we waited to run down all our doubts, it would flow past us. –*Learned Hand*

The Vietnam War was peaking when we were scheduled to go for our new carrier's first tour in the Vietnam War zone. We had a scheduled six-week training cruise to the Caribbean, and then four weeks back in Norfolk when everyone would be able to sell or store what they needed to, and then we would head to Vietnam for a year.

When we left Norfolk, we had barely gotten out of sight of land when we started recovering the aircraft from all of the squadrons based on the ship. It was a huge ship, with many squadrons and over one hundred aircraft, as well as five thousand five hundred people when the squadrons were aboard.

The mess halls (cafeterias) were open twenty-three hours a day, and there were at least eight different movies shown each night. It had basketball courts on the hangar deck, exercise rooms, and different stores where you could buy the things you needed for ship life. It also had a nice library. There were poker games going on all over the ship at almost any time. Even so, most sailors complained about being at sea because after duty, there was not that much to do.

At this time I was trying to read everything I could find by existentialist philosophers like Camus and Sartre, which I concluded were so dark and void of hope that they made ship life seem bright and beautiful. I had gotten to the existentialists by beginning with the Greeks and trying to follow the sequence of the development of philosophy, but concluded that most of this time had just been wasted. There just had to be more and better meaning to life than I could find with them, so I dropped philosophy and focused on another possible source for understanding the breakdowns my parents had—psychology and psychiatry.

I studied everything I could find by Freud, Jung, May, Fromm, B.F. Skinner, and eventually even R.D. Laing. Some of these had insights about what was wrong with people, but their solutions seemed somewhere between foolish and dangerous. Like the philosophers, it seemed their conclusions were far too comprehensive to be based on the little information or experience that the field had. Like philosophy, I felt that psychiatry was heading more into darkness than light, but I didn't have the light either.

R.D. Laing was particularly interesting, and in a unique way, encouraging to me. His basic premise was that if you are normal in this world you are crazy. That made sense to me, and would far more so in the weeks to come.

Laing also seemed to believe that maladies like schizophrenia were demonic. I was not sure what demons were at the time, but they were obviously invisible, supernatural beings, and bad ones that could control people. Many of the things he described sounded like what had happened to my parents, and maybe things we had experienced in the Caribbean. So I did not dismiss his theories, but did not fully understand them either.

So, at this young age I had gained a lot of knowledge, and some dangerous knowledge. Combined with the arrogance the accumulation of knowledge can lead to, I foolishly began trying to psychoanalyze everyone and the major events unfolding in the world as if the world itself was a person.

As my Chief at Gitmo had helped me learn how to share things with more wisdom, I would drop thoughts on the officers I was playing chess with that got their attention. Soon I was like the squadron junior guru/counselor. They would come and share personal and dark things in their life with me, and I would offer them advice. I may have helped some, but I think probably messed up more than I helped. But they kept coming back.

When I occasionally gave a diagnosis that a mental health professional had confirmed, I started getting bold trying to help people. Because I would maybe help one in ten just a little bit, I thought I could become a psychoanalyst. I was really becoming an idiot, and one day I was given the grace to see it.

To this day I am very wary of anyone who is not a professional, and even some professionals, who think they know other people's heart or motives. Professionals can do some good, and they can make people worse, but the amateur ones like I was are far more dangerous and can really get people messed up.

Even so, my studies on insanity fit in well with the late 1960s and 1970s. The whole world seemed to be going insane. One of the officers I played chess with boasted about how there were enough nukes just on our ship to destroy all life on earth, and enough in the entire U.S. Navy to destroy all life on earth at least twenty-five times. He said that if we add what the Air Force had we, the United States, could have wiped out all life on earth a hundred times.

Now think about that. I'm not sure what the point is after destroying all life on earth just once, but I guess we were threatening the Soviets with something like, "If you destroy me ten times, I'm going to destroy you fifty times!" It seemed over the top crazy, and we were to experience this crazy very close up just a few weeks into our deployment.

As we were sailing in the Caribbean on the short training cruise, I began to love being at sea. I played a lot of chess, but I also read for hours a day. At night some of us would lay in the nets that surrounded the flight deck and just gaze at the stars, which were spectacular when the ship was in black-out with no other lights around. With the gentle rocking of the ship up and down I think it may have been some of the best sleeping I'd ever had. It just seemed impossible that we were about to become the tip of the spear in a crisis that would become the closest mankind may have to a nuclear holocaust.

One night while lying in the nets the ship turned and accelerated. It was so abrupt that we knew something serious was up. The ship had five giant propellers about two stories high, and we could out run our task force just using two. I think they cranked up all five that night because it was hard to stand up on the flight deck. I went to the fantail and it looked like we were leaving a speed boat rooster tail behind us. We were being diverted to the Mediterranean on emergency orders to sail into a growing Middle East crisis.

We were told we were the first aircraft carrier to make it across the Atlantic without Soviet detection, but they picked us up immediately as we passed the Straights of Gibraltar. This began over four weeks of close encounters with the Soviet ships or aircraft virtually every day, and they weren't friendly ones.

The Soviet Navy and Air Force seemed especially intent on trying to provoke us into an incident. It came close to working a few times. One day a Soviet destroyer kept cutting in front of us while we were launching and recovering aircraft. We finally went after the little pest. Just before it seemed we would run over it, our ship turned hard and created a huge wave. The destroyer completely disappeared under it. I thought we had sunk it, but it bobbed up like a cork after being a submarine for a bit. That was the last Soviet ship that tried to do that to us again.

Once a Soviet Bear bomber came so close to us that it seemed its wing might scrape our flight deck. Two of our F-4

Phantom jet fighters were just about doing the same to it. These kinds of provocations were happening nearly every day. We all thought we were going to end up in a real battle. Then the ultimate scare came.

There were a number of elevators on the ship, each designated for certain things. Some were for ordinance—bombs and ammunition for the aircraft. One was specifically for the nuclear bombs, and everyone knew it was not to be used for anything else. When the announcement came over the ship's speakers that this elevator was active I think all of our hearts stopped. I went up to the flight deck to witness the nukes being loaded on to the "go birds." These were the planes on the catapults with engines running ready to be launched. It looked like I had a front row seat to the end of the world.

President Nixon later admitted in an interview that we had come closer to nuclear war during that crisis than at any time in our history, including the Cuban Missile Crisis. The Soviets had notified Nixon that they were going to destroy Israel, and Nixon replied that if they touched Israel we would count it as an attack on the U.S. and unleash everything we had at them. They backed down. Soon afterward the crisis was over.

Having witnessed my parents, who I had considered two of the wisest and most stable people, and then watch their sanity go so fast, I was not that trusting of the stability or sanity of anyone. I was far less trusting of anyone with the power to destroy the earth so many times over. It seemed during that crisis that the whole world was going the same way that my parents had, and instead of just wrecking a family, the whole world was at risk.

Everything I had been studying by supposedly the world's wisest and greatest thinkers did not leave me thinking that anyone was that wise. That day I began to seriously believe that the world was doomed. This would change the trajectory of my life.

So, while those above my pay grade were trying not to blow up the world, we had another crisis on the ship. We had only brought enough pot and other drugs on board to last for the six-week Caribbean training cruise. To remedy this, I went to one of the galleys where I knew some cooks, and we mixed up some oregano that looked and smelled like Hashish. At least it was close enough to fool those who used it. We cooked it and then started distributing it. It's amazing how stoned so many people got on oregano! It's a good thing they did too because you could get lost at sea for things like that.

After a few really intense weeks the destruction of all life on earth seemed to have been averted, at least for a while. I had a revelation from this I still believe—*every day that the world survives is a miracle.* It was obviously not our wisdom keeping us alive, so someone bigger than us was not letting our own madness destroy the world. I was sure it was someone, but I had no idea who.

I think when you expect to die soon just about everyone has some kind of religious inclination. Maybe this is magnified when you think everyone is about to die. I had always casually believed that there had to be a Creator, and whoever this was likely cared about His creation. I hoped to one day find out who this was, but nothing I had studied to date had been convincing. In fact, they had all been very unconvincing. There did not seem to be in any religion wisdom beyond human wisdom, and most of them came across like human fantasies. Still, I believed there had to be something or someone who created us.

As I said, at that point I had not even considered Christianity as an option. I had listened to a couple of Christians witness to me, but I couldn't connect with what they were saying. Even so, I knew that someone had to be looking out for us, keeping us from destroying ourselves. Everything I had learned through experience and my studies made it clear that if man was alone, we could never have gotten this far.

My religious experience after witnessing the world nearly being destroyed did not last long. Because of the inconvenience of not having the thirty days at home to sell or secure everything before leaving for Vietnam, but had been sent to the Mediterranean, and after the crisis told to stay and were assigned to the 6th fleet, the Navy wanted to do something nice for us. So, the rest of our deployment was like a pleasure cruise as we just went from port to port, and only had about three days of flight ops the rest of the time I was on the ship.

I think I got in some kind of trouble in every port. In Palma, Spain it became known somehow that I was a good chess player and I was challenged by a German doctor, who had also been a former Nazi doctor at one of the concentration camps. I played so much chess at sea that I did not want to spend my liberty time doing it, but I agreed to the match mostly out of curiosity.

My opponent had the air of aristocracy, but I liked him at first. Then he started telling me what he had done to prisoners in the concentration camps, including things like making lampshades out of their skin. I went from liking this seemingly polished gentleman to thinking he was the most despicable person I had ever met. I have never killed anyone, but if I had gone into that business, he would have been the first on my list. I just did not think anyone like him should be a member of the human race.

The good thing that came from meeting this man was I became interested in and began to study the Nazis, which I have continued to this day. I learned quickly that there was an ultimate evil that manifested through them that we must understand, and counter, or it will continue to devastate our world. It is the same spirit of racism that is now rising in our country again.

After feeling so slimed by this Nazi creep, I went to a party hosted by one of the fighter squadrons on our ship. The Nazi doc had mentioned that you could buy speed over the counter in any pharmacy there, so I stopped by one and loaded up to sell on the ship. It was not long before everyone in the squadron was plastered, so I went to each one and gave them a pill or two of this speed and told them it was something that would keep them from having a hangover. I was wanting to check it out to see how good it was, but I didn't want to take it myself. This seemed to be the solution.

It turned out to be good enough that when I went to their squadron sleeping quarters at about 3am, no one was asleep. They were all talking to each other about everything and anything—in the dark. I had never heard such a volume of chatter about nothing in my life.

In one port I was angered by how some pimps were treating their girls, and got a few friends together to run them off. They left fast, and I thought "that was easy." Then they returned with weapons. The Shore Patrol got there just in time or I don't know how we would have gotten out of that one.

In Athens, I barely escaped with my life. I had been led into a trap in an alley while buying some pot, but escaped the trap in a way that I still do not understand. I ran as fast as I could having no idea where I was going. I went down alleys and streets with police seemingly everywhere, and they were all after me. I turned one corner and the girl I was with had a taxi waiting and the door open. I jumped in and told the driver to go, and for some reason the police stopped and did not try to follow us. When I got back on board the ship I found out why.

The girl I had spent the last few days with happened to be the niece of one of the colonels who had taken over the country in a junta. The girl was from Chicago, and she had never told me anything about who her uncle was, but the trap had been to get me away from this girl. The authorities knew who I was and notified the ship about my attempt to purchase drugs.

My squadron commander ordered me to come to his stateroom, and he read me the request from the local Greek authorities for my extradition, and then read me his own riot act. I knew better than to admit to anything, especially trying to purchase illegal drugs. I was told my crime carried a thirty-year prison term in Greece at the time. However, I did admit to the skipper using pot while in the Navy. The skipper was not going to turn me over to the local authorities, but would handle it with a Captain's Mast. This is sort of a mini-trial before your commander who is the judge.

I was expecting to get busted in rank, and probably brig time, but what he gave me I would have paid a lot of money for. I was sent back to the States to be discharged from the Navy, but honorably so that I would not lose any of my G.I. benefits. It was like a dream come true. There was nothing I wanted more than to get out of the Navy at that time, and just like that I was going home.

It was getting very hard to be in the service at this time because of the growing anti-war and counter-culture movements. Some would even buy wigs to wear when they went home so that they would not be recognized as military. It was not uncommon in the States for those in uniform to be spit on, or occasionally get attacked physically. It is wonderful to see how the country's attitude towards the military has changed now, but then we seemed to be hated by our own country.

The Navy had been very good to me and for me, but when I could no longer work on the planes, playing chess all day was interesting, but my service seemed pointless. I needed to get out, but I now regret very much that I was not able to end my tour better. The Navy gave much more to me than I gave the Navy.

Almost all of my memories of the Navy now are of great people, great training, great places, and great experiences. The Navy even had great food. It also gave me an amazing amount of time to read and study. When I got out I had the G.I. Bill that paid for almost all of my flight training so that I was able to get an Airline Transport Rating. To be out and free was one of the best feelings I ever had. Even so, I did not know my life was about to go to a much higher level of excitement so fast.

If only we'd stop trying to be happy, we could have a pretty good time. *–Edith Wharton*

Chapter 10
Dropping Out

The man who aims at nothing is sure to hit it. *(Unknown)*

My older sister, Joanne, married Emmett Hailey. Everyone liked Emmett for his sense of humor, but he was also a serious, disciplined, hard worker. When he and Joanne saw me drifting toward the counter-culture after my discharge from the Navy, they invited me to come live with them in Richmond. Emmett had a union construction job at a nuclear power plant being built in Surry, Virginia, and he offered to get me on with the union as an apprentice pipe coverer.

This was my first and only experience working for a union, and it was a good one. The union demanded excellence and performance from every member. They prided themselves in giving the contractors the most that they could for what they were paid, and would kick out of the union any who were slack in their work.

It seemed all of the construction workers were serious about this, but they were also friendly, fun loving, and even though the work could be hard, I enjoyed it a lot. The "hard hats" as construction workers are called, had a comradery almost like being in the Navy. The pay was great too, and I was soon able to buy a motorcycle, which is all I wanted for transportation at the time.

We came home to Richmond on weekends and I became friends with several counter-culture groups from the Fan District. This is the artsy/student area around Virginia Commonwealth University.

I especially appreciated the way hippies accepted everyone as they were. Everyone was weird, so no one was weird. This meant that they even accepted straight people, as long as they weren't cops. At that time "straight" meant those who did not do drugs. There was rarely any kind of backbiting or critical judging of others. That was considered negative thinking and would bring you "down," or make you depressed. Our goal was to always stay high. It was superficial, but worked well most of the time.

It was curious how the hippie community that was so into peace and love had so many around it who were members of violent motorcycle gangs. When I learned that they controlled most of the drug business it made sense, but I had a hard time trusting them. Then, through a bizarre experience I became friends with some of the leaders of one of the most violent gangs.

The way this happened was one night three friends and I were going to a party in one of the high-rise apartment buildings. Just before reaching the door, a guy jumped out to block our path. He was a member of the Hells Angels who had come from California to establish some business contacts with the local gangs. I had met him before, but did not care for him, or trust him. He was pushy and obnoxious. For some reason this night he was being especially belligerent and wanted to pick a fight. He offered to take us all on at once, or one at a time.

I smirked so he rushed me and tried to kick me in the face. One of the things you learn in the military is how to fight. I dodged his kick and caught him with a hook that knocked him to the ground. I then jumped on him and bloodied him pretty badly until he escaped by rolling under a car.

When he crawled out from under the car a few minutes later and wanted to shake my hand, I refused. I was disgusted from getting blood all over my clothes, and threatened to punish him more if he did not leave. I had no idea how close this would come to getting me killed.

Later that night I was at a popular psychedelic nightclub when it sounded like thunder surrounding the building. A girl came running over to me saying the Confederate Angels were outside and they were looking for me. It was obvious they had covered all of the escapes, so I decided to walk out the front door and face them. There seemed to be two leaders, and they were huge. Worse, they had chains and sawed-off shotguns.

I tried to be as composed as I could when I walked up to them and asked why they were looking for me. They asked if I had gotten into a fight with the Hells Angel who was standing nearby. I said I had. Then they asked if I had refused to shake his hand after the fight. Discerning the problem, I said I would shake it now, and went over and did. Then the leaders came over to shake my hand, saying they hated that guy and were glad I had kicked his ___. Then others came over to greet me too. Just like that I was not only accepted, but was being celebrated.

Later one of them explained what an offense it is to motorcycle gangsters to not shake hands after a fight. They assured me that they would have killed me if I had not shaken the man's hand, even though they hated him and was glad I had done it. This gang had a reputation for being killers, and I did not doubt that this was true.

When we parted they actually said that if I ever needed their help to let them know, and gave me a contact number. Whenever I saw them around after that, they were very friendly.

This was dramatic, but it showed to me how in this strange world something very small can turn a person from being an enemy into a friend, or turn a friend into an enemy.

Even the best relationships can be hard. What makes something a treasure is that it is either rare, or hard to find. True friends are treasures. Most of us only have so much time and energy to invest in relationships, but true friendships are worth the investment. Even the best friendships still have ups and downs. Relationships are something we must learn to navigate, and will spend our life navigating, so we need to understand what's required for a good relationship.

There is a factor that one of my friends expressed that can help when navigating relationships. We called it PAC for "People Are Crazy." I think this has well proven itself to be true. We all do crazy things, so we should not be overly upset when others do. Didn't all of Jesus' best friends go a bit crazy at the end? He knew it was coming, and was ready to receive them back without penalty. Forgiving as much as we can is about the only way we can keep friendships, so we must resolve up front that this is going to be required.

Continuing with the PAC principle, and understanding that I'm also one who has done many crazy things, it was during this time in my life when my highest ambition was to go to every rock festival. At this I became a success.

The rock festivals were the best parties of all, especially the ones that lasted for days. Because the anti-war demonstrations in Washington usually had rock concerts as part of them to draw people for the demonstrations, even when I was not that political I would go, as would most of my friends. Please understand that this was BC (before Christ) and rock festivals became the highlight of my life at this time.

At one of the bigger demonstrations in Washington I ended up at a Marxist rally. I'm not sure how that happened, but what usually drew me to a group back then was either the drugs or girls. I had studied Marxism while in the Navy, reading all that I could find by the top Marxist thinkers. After reading *The Capitalist* by Karl Marx, I considered it somewhere between foolish and madness, but I think I was typical of most of those from the counter-culture, or those who hung out on the fringes of it.

Even so, I thought it was incredible that so many in the world could believe something so ridiculous, but as I saw at this rally, almost all were Marxists as a rebellion, and really did not know what they were talking about with either the economics or politics of Marxism. I hung around this group for a time anyway, and saw a lot about what was really going on with the demonstrations, which according to those I know who have been in the ones that have begun to rock our country again, are the same today as they were then.

At these demonstrations there were always some who were professional agitators, and most of these were the Marxists. Having settled into the laid back, accept everyone hippie lifestyle, I didn't like the way the Marxist speakers were always raging, trying to get everyone mad at the government, or the "establishment," especially the capitalists, the military-industrial complex, or a myriad of other institutions. They did not have a vision, and never spoke about the positives of Marxism, which any thinking person who studies Marxism soon learns is because there aren't any. Marxism is about destroying, not building. They claim to be building a utopia, but it is so vaguely defined, and their strategy for doing it is basically tear down all present institutions and governments, and then seemingly just expect the utopia to magically appear.

Because I read so much, and was accumulating knowledge about many things, I was becoming arrogant, but also disillusioned about almost everything at the time. For this reason, I could understand the anger of the Marxists, but with a few exceptions they were hard to like. Since to me it looked like the world was going to blow up soon anyway, I thought the best thing to do was have as good a time as possible. So I became pretty shallow in my political or other convictions, except for being a dedicated hedonist. If I became political during this period of my life it was for reasons other than politics.

Please allow me to interject one more thing here about the basics of Marxism. Marx was considered by virtually everyone who knew him well to be the most despicable person they had ever met. The main reason no one could bear him was that he could not tolerate anyone questioning anything he said. Those who questioned him he would not just reject, but seek to destroy them. He considered himself to be the greatest genius of all, and was outraged when anyone had the audacity to question anything he said, or did not comply completely with his demands. His rage at the world was based on the world's failure to recognize his genius and fail to bow to him.

Yet, Marx's theories on human nature, politics, and economics were so ridiculous that even a ten-year-old that could think for themselves would see through them. Now think about the nature of Marxism. In every place it is imposed absolutely no questioning of Marxism or the Marxist authorities can be tolerated without the most draconian reprisals, often imprisonment or death.

In short, Marxists take on the spirit of Marx in their intolerance of any debate or challenge. Therefore, they become the most humorless and despicable people to be around, just like Marx. Because Marxism has now deeply infiltrated the American institutions of education, the media, and entertainment (the three main targets that Marxist strategists declared to be their main targets that would allow them to take over America) we see that those now have become the most intolerant of any debate or challenge. This extreme intolerance is one of the most basic signs of where some form of Marxism has gotten into the mix.

There is no humor or joy in Marxism. Yet, we see that some of the Scandinavian socialist countries have been called the best countries to live in and the happiest. Really? First, you can make a poll say anything you want it to by the questions you ask, and who you ask. Then we need to consider whose definition of happiness we're going to use. If these people are so happy why do they have the highest suicide rates? Why do the people in them seem so generally depressed?

I have spent a lot of time in Scandinavia, and I do know some happy people in Scandinavian countries. You can find some happy people in socialist countries, even communist countries like Cuba, but they are rare exceptions. There are some exceptional people in every country and culture, but in general, the most depressed countries are socialists or communists. People were created to be free and to have real joy, and those two almost always go together.

Now back to my story. As the Marxists were the least enjoyable people to be around, seemingly always bitter or angry, so I drifted from them pretty quickly. Through much of the Cold War it did seem that Marxism had a shot at taking over the world, but I was convinced the world would be destroyed first. I knew I could not bear to live under a Marxist/socialist state, so I set out to just enjoy life while I could before the world was destroyed, or subdued by Marxists.

Staying stoned helped me escape from the realities that otherwise only led to anxiety. Because I had seen what fear had done to my mother, I was especially concerned about fear creeping into my life. For this reason, I only did soft drugs. I had tried speed, in the form of tablets you could buy over the counter in Europe. It was a sensational high, but when you came off of the high you became paranoid. I saw the same happen to heroin or coke users too, so I stayed away from those drugs out of a fear of fear.

Addicted people also became intolerably self-centered and untrustworthy. I had some I considered very close friends steal from me to support their habit—you could not leave anything of value around them. I watched some of the most interesting people become boring and dark, depressed shells of their former selves. The fear of becoming these things kept me from doing hard drugs. I was still visionless and directionless, but I was having a pretty good time. I was proving the quote at the beginning of this chapter: "The man who aims at nothing is sure to hit it."

All of this time I still intended to be a writer, but I had no idea what to write about. My favorite authors were the Russian classics like Tolstoy, Dostoevsky, and Chekov, or American authors like Norman Mailer and C.T. Stud. Then I ran into Tom Wolfe, and read his *Electric Kool-Aid Acid Test.*

Tom Wolfe described our lifestyle at the time about as well as it could be done. He was brilliant, articulate, and had a subtle but insightful humor. He wrote in such a way that you never wanted his books to end. They took you on an interesting, exciting journey that was constantly entertaining. He may be one of the best writers of all-time for style, but did not have much of a message. His books were valuable for helping you understand different types of people and current trends, but that was about it.

Tragically, some of the best writers don't have much to say, and some who have a lot to say are not very good writers. The classics are those that are both powerfully articulate and have a powerful message. I wanted to write something significant, something that would have an impact, and leave the reader with a feeling of being taken to a new destination. But I did not have the patience to develop the ability to articulate like a Tom Wolfe. At that time I had some knowledge of many things, but deep convictions about none.

I didn't know where I was going. I was living an enjoyable life, but not a meaningful one. At the time I didn't want to change that. I wanted to stay on the bus like in *The Electric Kool-Aid Acid Test*, but I wanted my writing to be different. That doesn't work, so I wrote a lot, but would throw it away because it was not worth keeping. Even so, the practice of writing would help me later. In God's economy nothing is wasted.

One of the enjoyable things I did at this time was to visit the Peachers. They were my favorite family and like a mooring to some normality, even though they were not that normal. I say that in a positive way, considering R.D. Laing's hypothesis that if you are normal in this world you are crazy.

I would often spend an evening with the Peachers watching sitcoms and listening to Alice's opinions on just about everything. Her penny ante games were as raucous as ever, and watching her watch sports was more entertaining than the games we were watching.

Another friend that grew up on our street, David Atkins, also discovered the Peachers. David added to the entertainment because he would actually argue with Alice and try to change her opinions. I know she came close to smacking him a few times, and I wanted to be there to see it when it did happen.

One time David and Alice were going at it about something, and David just blurted out, "You're stupid, woman!" As soon as he said this he knew he had made a very bad mistake. Alice jumped out of her seat and charged. I'm pretty sure she was intent on beating the crap out of him. I saw terror in David's eyes. He flew out the door and ran down the street as fast as he could, with Alice right on his heels. He barely got away.

For about a year after this David would not even risk coming into the Peacher's yard. Occasionally he would stand in the street and yell for Bart, Bonnie, or me if he wanted to talk to us. If Alice appeared at the door he would bolt. You kind of have to know both of those characters to really appreciate it, but this ongoing battle was great entertainment.

Even though partying almost every night, and basically living a life of no real responsibility may sound great, it got old. When I read a psychological study that concluded that any human being deprived of meaningful labor would go insane, I believed it. We were made to accomplish something. To live such a directionless, meaningless life that is really not accomplishing anything is a road to madness.

A man can fail many times, but he is not a failure until he begins to blame someone else. *–John Burroughs*

Chapter 11
New Horizons

The greatest mistake you can make in life is continually fearing you'll make one. *–Elbert Hubbard*

My family, except for Joanne, had all moved to Raleigh, N.C. I decided to visit them. While there, I met some interesting people that were a little different breed of hippie/dropout. They smoked a lot of pot and did some psychedelics, but they didn't just sit around and "groove" while stoned—they went out and did things. They had vision for their lives and were doing things to accomplish them, not just wasting away. I liked them so much I decided to stay in Raleigh for a while.

Several of us rented a big house together. There was almost a continuous party going on there, but the house was big, and we had our own rooms, so we could get away if needed. It was a very enjoyable situation.

At the time, I was trying to set up a network for LSD distribution on the East Coast. I was dealing with some guys from Britain who were suppliers for the music scene there. They made the best products, so a part of my being responsible and accomplishing something was to help make them more available in the U.S. The problem was that these suppliers would often get paranoid and disappear for weeks at a time.

While waiting for these guys to get un-paranoid and make the deal, I got a part-time job at a well-known jazz club called "The Frog and the Nightgown." I got to meet some of the great jazz musicians like Stan Getz, as well as some that would soon become big like Bette Midler and Barry Manilow.

Barry was playing keyboards for Bette Midler, and at the time had only written one hit, but it was a big one—the McDonald's jingle *"Have you had a break today?"* Years later I heard him say that he had made more money off of that jingle than any other hit, and he had some big hits.

So the people I met at this club were great party people, but also achievers. They did not just get stoned and listen to music, they got stoned and wrote music. These were doers, not just dreamers. Our house became one of the go to party houses when they came to play at The Frog and Nightgown. They liked to have a good time, but also worked hard at their craft every day. This helped me to get some traction with my life and begin doing something. I think we were becoming a new breed of hippies with ambition.

Mary

If you trust, you will be disappointed occasionally, but if you mistrust, you will be miserable all the time. *–Abraham Lincoln*

I don't recall how or where I met Mary, but it was likely at The Frog and Nightgown. She remains one of the most unique people I have known. I had no idea the impact she would have on the trajectory of my life. She was not a part of the counter-culture, but was a very straight girl who might occasionally smoke a joint. She was a high school Spanish teacher, and lived with her mother in a modest but nice little house near the NC State campus.

Mary was a beautiful girl, but there was far more to her than physical beauty. Mary was confident, but not arrogant. She was intelligent and could be really interesting. She put on no airs, and is one of the most profoundly honest people I've known.

To begin with our relationship was just physical. I had no idea it would become more than that, but it did not take me long to start really enjoying her company. She had suffered tragedies in her life, but did not seem to be scarred by them. She liked a good party, but was not going to waste her life in them. I had never met anyone with as much physical charm, and so much substance and depth. It was not long before we were spending almost every evening together, and not long after that when we were semi-living together.

Mary and I started getting serious enough that I took her to Richmond to meet the Peachers. I knew she would love them, and she did, especially Alice. However, I should have better prepared her for Alice. Alice took Mary into the kitchen and started to ask some questions about our relationship. Mary, being so honest and transparent, started out with what a great physical relationship we had and did so with far too much detail. Bart overheard some of it and came to get me in a panic saying, "You've got to stop her!"

When I got to the kitchen, I had never seen Alice in such shock, and Mary was just going on like this was normal. To this day that remains the only time I think I ever saw Alice speechless. That was typical Mary. She would even talk to her mother about such things just as openly. She was maybe too transparent at times, but without guile.

Mary had met The Lord, been born again and baptized in The Spirit while in college. She walked with The Lord for about thirty days, and then she just told Him that she wanted to experience some other things for a time, but would be back to serve Him later. She was just as honest and straightforward with God.

When I met some of Mary's friends from college they told amazing stories about her. She had started going to a house church meeting at the home of one of her professors, just out of curiosity. After weeks of attending she had become convinced that they were real, and The Lord was real.

Having been amazed at the gifts of The Spirit that were often demonstrated at these meetings, but not really sure if she wanted to get so serious with God yet, she started telling her friends about these meetings, and then would bring them to one so that they could get born again and baptized in The Spirit. Then Mary would ask them what it was like so she could determine if she wanted to do it or not.

Mary led quite a few people to The Lord like this before she took the leap herself. She loved it and loved God, but as related above, after thirty days of walking with The Lord she told Him she would be back later. She was too honest to do anything halfway. For her it would be all in or nothing, and she was not yet ready for the total commitment.

Eventually Mary shared some things with me about her experience with The Lord. I had met a few people who were Christians, but none that seemed to be as sure as she did that Jesus was God and that The Bible is true. I could not imagine knowing this as deeply as she did and not following Him, but she was confident and excited about the time when she would.

I also knew that Mary was honest to a fault, and would never say things like this she did not absolutely believe. This made me want to hear more about her experiences and the miracles she had witnessed. I took what she shared seriously, and for the first time I can remember I started to believe in Jesus myself, at least to the degree that I could. I got a Bible and started to read it and could not believe that with all of the books I had read I had skipped this one! I believed everything I read in it.

Being convinced intellectually is still not the same as having your own experience with Him. When Mary told me about how The Lord still did miracles for His people, and that you just needed have faith that He would when praying, I started praying with as much faith as I could muster for the LSD deal to work out. It worked out so quickly I really thought God had answered my prayer. So, I started praying for other deals. I also started becoming an evangelist as I told my friends how God answered prayer, and how He did this for my drug deal.

Now I'm not saying The Lord answered that prayer, but I had no concept of righteousness, holiness, or anything else about Christ. I had heard that He would forgive our sins, but I didn't know what sins were. I believed that He was real, and that He would do for us what we asked for with faith. I was not born again, did not have His Spirit, but I was trying to get to know Him, and thought I was doing pretty good at it.

I was not trying to be trifling with God, but I was ignorant. I also think The Lord may have answered my prayer to make the LSD deal because I got it the day before I was born again and baptized in His Spirit. I ended up going home and flushing all of that acid down the toilet. I'm just sayin…

And just to say a little about ignorance here, studies have revealed that a high percentage of youth today that have been raised in evangelical churches are about as ignorant of such things as I was because they have never been taught the meaning of sin, immorality, or impurity.

First Vision

Mystical experiences, like those that marked my childhood, are apparently far from rare. –*Albert Hofmann*

Before my conversion, one night Mary and I were staying at a hotel on a beach when I looked out over the ocean and saw a white fiery chariot with horses passing by maybe a hundred feet off the water. At first I thought the pot we'd smoked must have been laced with something psychedelic. I did not tell Mary anything about this vision until later that night because I could not get the image out of my head.

Mary thought I had seen Elijah's chariot. I knew nothing about Elijah or his chariot, but she seemed to think this meant I had some kind of calling on my life with God. I liked the idea that God would have some purpose for me, but I didn't really know what that meant.

At this time, I was still trying to get traction with what I was going to do with my life. I was determined to be a writer, but still had nothing inspiring to write about. This thought of having a "calling" or a purpose started to get my attention. I hoped it was true, and started getting very interested in getting to know about God, and perhaps writing about Him. How could there be anything more interesting than knowing God? I had no trouble thinking about spending the rest of my life studying Him and writing about Him.

I had never had a vision, didn't really know what they were, and later would wrestle with the thought that it had just been my imagination. Now that I understand visions I know that I did see that chariot, though I'm not sure it was Elijah's. Imaginations disappear fast, but I can to this day still remember what that chariot looked like. It would be a few years before I understood it, but the immediate result was that it sowed in me the thought that I had a calling, a purpose from God. Of all the things I had ever dreamed of doing, this was by far the best, and I had to pursue it.

Live as if you were to die tomorrow. Learn as if you were to live forever. *–Gandhi*

Extra effort wins games. It builds businesses, it amasses fortunes, it wins battles. Talent may be inherited but effort is acquired. –*R. Redwine*

Chapter 12
Reality

When it is dark enough, you can see the stars. *–Ralph Waldo Emerson*

At this same time when I'm just starting to believe that there is a God and Jesus is His Son, and I might even have a calling but I'm still really ignorant of Him and the entire spiritual realm, I ran into a couple of girls who claimed to be witches. I had no idea how radically my life would be changed by this.

In the counter-culture community it seemed everyone was claiming to be something weird or outrageous, so claiming to be a witch was not that uncommon. Then they told me that they were on their way to a séance where they would make demons appear. They explained that demons were powerful supernatural beings that they could control for things like casting spells or curses on people. I thought they were just doing too many drugs, but agreed to go with them because I was just getting interested in the whole spiritual and supernatural thing.

The séance was weird, but when the demons appeared I was shocked and terrified. I knew instinctively that they were evil, they were powerful, and the girls were not controlling them, but they were controlling the girls.

I left as fast as I could. I now knew for sure that there was a really evil supernatural, so I reasoned that if there was evil there had to be a good supernatural to at least hold the evil in check. What I had learned about Jesus—He must be it. Seeing the chariot had not been very disturbing, but seeing these creatures was terrifying. I never wanted to see anything like that again.

I told Mary about this experience, and she gave me the biggest download on Jesus ever. She then decided to move back to her mom's. I think the demon thing really freaked her out. I started reading the New Testament with renewed devotion, and was surprised to see all of the references to demons. I had started becoming a believer, but seeing the evil supernatural made me feel that this was an ultimate life and death kind of serious, and not just for me, but the whole world.

War of the Worlds

When you're going through hell, keep going. *–Winston Churchill*

Then one night I woke up and felt a presence in the room. Living in that party house I first thought one of the guests must have drifted into my room by mistake. When I looked up, I saw the demons that had appeared in the séance, and they were reaching out their hands toward me. Mary had told me that even demons would flee at the name of Jesus, so I used His name, and it worked! They disappeared so fast I knew His name had terrified them.

I was excited to share this with Mary. To me, it proved even more that Jesus was all she thought He was. I was thrilled that His name was so powerful. I think Mary was still debating about whether this was the time to go "all in" for Him, but I was sure I was. I started reading The Bible every chance I got. I could hardly believe what a great story it was.

I also started wanting to experience what Mary had told me about—how Jesus was still doing all of the same things that He did when He walked the earth, only now He was doing them through His people. I wanted to meet these people and become one of them. In fact, I don't think I had ever wanted anything as much as I wanted this. But the devil had other plans, and there was about to be a war over my soul. After the battle that was coming I would know for sure that there was no turning back.

The demons started coming back to my room every few nights, then every night, and then several times a night. Every time I used the name of Jesus, they would depart, but they were coming back faster and more determined. They were always reaching for me, and I thought that if they touched me I would die. I was getting sleep deprived and desperate. I did not want to alarm Mary any more than I already had, but I had no one else to talk to about this, so I told her all that was happening to me.

Mary said she would take me to see the "real Christians" she knew who had the house church in Greenville. I wanted to go right away. I did not think I would survive another night if I didn't. The battle in my mind was reaching a point where I knew this could not go on.

When we got to her former professor's house, a meeting was going on, so we sat in the back. I had never heard such beautiful singing. Many seemed enraptured in what they were doing. It was like having stepped into a whole different realm. I had never seen such joyful people. I started to feel an incredible peace, and my mind started to calm down.

Then I heard voices inside of me. They began to say things like, "These are God's people, but you're not one of them. You belong to us and tonight you are going to kill yourself." This voice spoke with such authority I thought that I was indeed going to kill myself that night. I was distraught. It seemed that what had been appearing to me had somehow gotten inside of me, and I was powerless to resist them.

The worst thing of all was seeing God's people like this, but being told I was not one of them. I thought that if I tried to speak all manner of evil might come out of my mouth, so I just cried out to God in my heart to help me.

Then I looked up and saw one of the older men in the front looking right at me. When we locked eyes, he stood up and walked back to where I sat. As he looked down at me, he laid his hand on my forehead. At first I felt a terrible rage rise up in me at this, but I think I was feeling what the intruders inside of me were feeling. Then the peace came back.

The man turned out to be one of the elders of this house church. He began to tell me how I had "seen Satan," and described the battle that I had been going through. He said that it had all happened because of my pride, and this was far truer than he could have possibly known. He then led me through a prayer to renounce my sin, and then renounce the evil one. I did it all with about as much sincerity as I'd ever done anything before. He then led me in a prayer to give my life to Jesus.

In just those few minutes I had gone from hell to heaven. I felt the evil leave me. Then I had never felt such joy before. I knew that I did belong to The Lord! I was one of His people! Just a few minutes before, I was sure that I would die that night, and now I felt like I was just beginning the greatest and happiest life I could ever live. I had taken many feel-good drugs in my life, but nothing I had ever experienced was as great as I felt that night.

Then several others walked over and laid hands on me. They were praying in what I had come to understand were "other tongues," or other languages given to them by The Spirit. Then they prayed in English for me to be baptized in The Holy Spirit. I did not think that I could have felt any better than I already did, but this took me even higher. I almost felt like I was sitting in The Lord's lap. He was all around me, and in me. This is what euphoria really meant.

Someone gave me a Bible. I opened it and the first verses my eyes fell on were Luke 10:17-20:

> **The seventy returned with joy, saying, "Lord, even the demons are subject to us in Your name."**
>
> **He said to them, "I was watching Satan fall from heaven like lightning.**
>
> **"Behold, I have given you authority to tread on serpents and scorpions, and over all the power of the enemy, and nothing will injure you.**
>
> **"Nevertheless do not rejoice in this, that the spirits are subject to you, but rejoice that your names are recorded in heaven."**

I felt that everything I had just read was for me and came straight from God. The words the people around me were speaking were words straight from Him. There is no describing how great this felt, especially after the torment I had just been through. I had given my life to God, and He had given me His Holy Spirit.

I was so caught up in the anointing of The Holy Spirit that I don't remember much about the rest of that night, or riding back to Raleigh with Mary. It was indescribable ecstasy. I felt that the car was full of angels, and as terrifying as the demons had been, The Holy Spirit, the angels, and everything I was feeling just then were overwhelmingly more wonderful and more powerful than the demons were.

I had entered a new world of the supernatural. I knew that my whole life I had been ignorant of this major factor that was likely controlling the world more than men were, and had been controlling me too. Now I wanted to be controlled by God. It took me some time to understand that He does not control people, but leads them by His Spirit. He is above manipulation and control—He only wants those loyal to Him to be so from their hearts, because they want to. God is the ultimate Liberator, and "where The Spirit of The Lord is there is liberty."

For the next few months, my life was a glorious whirlwind. Mary and I drifted apart. She was still debating whether it was time to go "all in" with God, and I could not even imagine not doing this. As much as I loved Mary, after all that she had just witnessed, for her to have hesitancy to go all in with The Lord caused me to question our future together. I would always appreciate what she had done to lead me to The Lord, but I knew it was time to move on from our relationship, and we did.

I had never even considered that life could be so good after that night. Who could even conceive of God not just moving in our life, but moving into our life? He lived in me! I was experiencing Him every day. I was living my own Book of Acts, in awe and wonder at the great things He was doing. I felt like I had found "the mother lode" of knowledge and wisdom, and of course I had found far more than that—I had found Life Himself. It was incomprehensible to me to do anything but follow Him.

**It is never too late to be what you might have been.
–*George Eliot***

Chapter 13
The Adventure Begins

Although the world is very full of suffering, it is full also of the overcoming of it. –Helen Keller

My life after being born again became so rich and meaningful it seemed that I had been living in a black and white world and suddenly saw color. Learning about God was much more interesting than anything I had studied before. The greatest sorrow I had was that I had not come to know Him much earlier—that I had spent so much of my life studying subjects that were so trivial.

So, I studied God like I had to make up for all of the lost time, hours a day, and when I did not have to work, just about all day. I could not get enough. I got a small pocket Bible to take to work so I could read it on breaks. I studied every minute I could get because it was the most interesting and fulfilling thing I had ever done.

I was told about a Christian bookstore in town. I was surprised that there was such a thing. It was like there was a whole Christian world that I had not known anything about. Christians hung out at the bookstore and virtually all of the conversation was about God and the great things He was doing. Ministry seemed to always be going on there, and people getting saved, healed, and delivered daily at the bookstore.

I started looking for the Christian bookstores everywhere I went. They were like an extension of church, and were in some ways probably more like church is intended to be. Not only could The Lord move there freely at any time, but people connected more deeply with each other than they could in the typical church it seemed, except for maybe the house churches. Some bookstores had soda fountains and sitting areas that were intended to promote fellowship and ministry, and they always seemed to be full of people.

The Christian bookstore was also the place to find out anything significant happening in the local body of Christ. Mary had told me that the "real Christians" met in houses like they did in the Book of Acts. So, at least for a time, I had a prejudice against any other kind of church and tried to find out where all of the house churches were in our area. There was a Christian bookstore in Raleigh called "The Sign of the Fish" for the ancient Christian symbol that believers would use to let others know they were in the faith. The owner of this bookstore seemed to know every house church in Raleigh and almost everything that was happening in them. This wasn't gossip, but was a kind of news service.

So, I made the rounds to these house churches. Each one seemed to me to be remarkable in its own way. It was hard for me to believe a movement this big and exciting was happening and everyone did not know about it. There did not seem to be a single meeting when we didn't leave knowing God had been there and had done something remarkable.

Most house churches met once or twice a week, but on any day of the week you could find at least one meeting. I put together a schedule so that I could go to one every night, and on Sundays I often went to one on Sunday morning and another Sunday night. When your experience with church life is the boring kind that I had as a child this may sound crazy, but when God is really moving in them there is nothing more exciting.

I went back occasionally to Doug and Dixie Ray's house church in Greenville where I had been delivered, born again, and baptized in The Spirit. I got water baptized by Doug and Dr. MacAndrews, the elder who prayed for me that first night. They also took some time to teach me some of the basic Christian doctrines and basic church life. They encouraged me to visit house churches overseen by a man they called an "apostle," Col. Doug Carty. The bookstore in Raleigh knew about him, and gave me directions to the house churches in the area that were associated with him. He came to Raleigh once a month to teach, and I tried to be there for all of them.

Col. Carty was retired from the Air Force, had a serious military demeanor, and a resolute devotion to The Scriptures and sound doctrine. It was this devotion that led him to believe that house churches were the only biblical model for church. I don't remember Col. Carty ever speaking against the institutional churches, but would emphasize that we should be devoted to doing everything according to the Scriptures, especially our church life.

My short Christian experience with church life confirmed what Col. Carty taught. I had met some very good Christians at the bookstore who went to more traditional churches, and they encouraged me to check out their churches too, which I did. I did not find in any of them anywhere close to the life in the house churches, but I was so new to the faith that I loved any teaching or preaching, but the rest of the service seemed too stiff and formal for my liking. So, for a few years I stuck with the house churches. Later I had some very spectacular experiences with God in more traditional churches, which caused me to lighten up a bit and begin to love them too.

To Fly Away or Stay

Life is made up of a series of judgments on insufficient data, and if we waited to run down all our doubts, it would flow past us. –*Learned Hand*

Everything about Christianity and the church was interesting to me. I hardly had to buy any books at that time because people gave me so many. One book being talked about so much that I had to read was *The Late Great Planet Earth* by Hal Lindsey.

Few books in history have had the impact on the Christian world as much as this one for a time. It had a similar impact on my life as well. For a time at least, a main topic of discussion for Christians was the rapture. For a time we wondered almost every day if that would be the day it happened. Many were using that book as an evangelistic tool, and it worked! Great numbers of people were being added to the faith from reading this book.

Though Hal Lindsey woke many sleeping Christians and caused many to come to The Lord, his teaching on the rapture would eventually be challenged by many teachers and Bible scholars. Some think it did more harm to the church than good, mostly by fomenting an escape mentality in Christians, causing them to fail to be the salt and light we are called to be now. Perhaps, and I could see even then why some would question some of its teaching. I think this book did a great deal of good overall.

Personally, I was happy for the rapture to come at any time, or glad to stay and do what I was called to do. Life in The Lord was far better than anything I had imagined. I was not that thrilled about leaving this life, but at the same time to go straight to heaven and start experiencing that was certainly a draw. I saw so much that needed to be done, and could be done, I just decided to focus on being here. If the rapture came, of course I would be fine with it, but it started falling to the bottom of my concerns.

Thanks to Col. Carty and other teachers of the time, I started to get a vision for what the glorious bride of Christ was called to be. This was a sustaining vision that gave me practical things to do and live for. I became very intent on learning what I could do to help the bride be ready for The Lord when He did come. This began in the first year of my life in The Lord, and has continued as a main focus of my life since.

Revival Fire

You never change things by fighting the existing reality. To change something, build a new model that makes the existing model obsolete. *–R. Buckminster Fuller*

One of the reasons that I learned this extraordinary and explosive new world of Christianity had been hidden from me was that it did not exist that way until about the time that I was converted. There was a huge wave of new believers coming into the faith through what would become known as "The Jesus People Movement" and "The Charismatic Movement." Both of these were peaking right about the time I became a believer. These two movements combined had one of the biggest impacts on Western Christianity than any revival or movement since The Reformation.

Some studies concluded that nearly as many new believers had come into the faith, more churches were planted, and more missionaries sent out just in the Charismatic Movement than in all previous movements in church history combined. Of course, this is due to more people being alive now than in history, but it did seem like the world was exploding with the knowledge and activity of God at that time.

As much as these two movements were different from each other, in powerful ways they complemented each other. The Jesus Movement was impacting the counter-culture movements. The Charismatic Movement was reaching people who were already in institutional churches, but had not been born again or baptized in The Holy Spirit. Soon dropouts and CEOs were sitting next to each other in all kinds of different Christian meetings and events. They got to know each other and became more than friends—they became brothers and sisters in the body of Christ.

When The Spirit is moving like He was then it seemed that we could talk to someone about the weather and they would ask how to be saved. It took me a while to understand that this was not normal church life. I had come to The Lord at a special time, and just assumed this was the way Christianity had been since the first century. Again, we tend to see the world the way we are, not as it is.

My conclusion now is that this kind of revival is more like church life as it is intended to be than what the church has often settled for. As I read the Book of Acts then it seemed to be close to what we were experiencing. This continues to be my understanding of what normal church life is supposed to be—it should be by far the most exciting thing in our life, as well as in the world.

This being said, it is reasonable that just as the pillar of cloud and fire would at times stop to allow Israel to rest, there are times when The Spirit has us park in one place for a time. However, that does not mean that our love for and excitement about God should level off. In fact, when movement in the church overall slows for a time that is when our personal excitement and relationship with God should grow the most.

The first personal healing I experienced was from what I believe to have been an ulcer. It was a stomach pain worse than I had ever experienced. It lasted for days, and was getting worse. I went to a house church meeting at the home of Jack and Gloria Simonds in Raleigh hoping to get prayer. I sat in the back waiting until the end of the meeting to ask the elders to pray for me, which I had been taught to do. However, during the worship one of the leaders interrupted the meeting to say someone had a serious stomach problem they needed to pray for right away. I raised my hand, they prayed for me, and the pain left immediately. Then the meeting continued.

This kind of thing was normal in the house churches then. If you had a physical problem your first thought was not to go to the doctor, but to go to church. We expected to be healed, and usually were. At the time testimonies of healing seemed to be as common as testimonies of salvation. Deliverance was a part of our church life too, and many of the physical healings were the result of a deliverance.

The Devil Returns

I've lived through some terrible things in my life, some of which actually happened. *–Mark Twain*

Months after I had committed my life to The Lord I was still living in the hippie party house. The others in the house did not mind, and neither did I. They called me a "Jesus freak," but to them everyone was some kind of freak, and they seemed fine with me being this kind of freak. I spent hours talking to them about what had happened to me and what I was learning.

They seemed to believe it, and be okay with it, for me. Later I was able to lead some of these friends into their own experience with The Lord.

As I studied The Bible and talked to other Christians about Christian behavior, I learned more about the sanctified life. I did my best to live it. I was challenged by all of it, especially with sexual immorality, but I was determined to live a pure life until married. This required that Mary and I not see each other anymore, and I resolved to stay out of tempting situations. This was hard, especially when I was still living in the party house.

I was so excited about God that I was determined to live a life that pleased Him. I had more peace and joy in my life than I had ever experienced, and every day was filled with wonder. I did not want to do anything to jeopardize what I was now experiencing. I've now been in the faith for fifty years and have to admit that some of the requirements of a sanctified life are still hard to live. What has kept me has not been trying to follow a set of rules, but rather loving God and living to get ever closer to Him as He promises we can do.

In the first few months of my Christian life it seemed to be supernatural how beautiful temptresses would show up at times. I did not pass all of these tests, and would feel terrible for a long time when I failed. I had not yet been taught about all of the trials and tests Christians must go through, and though I never doubted who The Lord was after the night I was born again, I started to doubt myself.

Though I had resisted many temtations, I had been going through a terrible struggle with my thoughts, and could not bring them all under subjection as I had read that we should. I started feeling very unsanctified, and was thinking I had something really wrong with me. This was troubling but became even more so when a few nights later the demons appeared again.

It was a terrible shock. I thought they were gone for good. I used the name of Jesus and they fled, but I was shaken by this. I had read what Jesus said about demons go out of a person, but always seek to return, if they do not find their old home occupied by The Holy Spirit. I started to wonder if maybe The Spirit had left me for all of my unholy thoughts and the times I had stumbled. King David had prayed and begged God not to take His Spirit from him, and I did the same.

Then the demons came back again. This time I could hear their thoughts as if they were spoken audibly. They said that I was still theirs and not The Lord's. This was my worst fear—that I had been rejected by God and turned back over to them. I literally started wanting to die if I could not walk with The Lord.

Then one night I felt a presence in the room, and quickly turned over to confront the demons. It was Jesus standing in the corner of my room. There were high ceilings in the old house, and He was elevated about two feet off the floor so that He was looking down at me. We locked eyes for about a minute. I felt like I was seeing perfect love. He then walked toward me, and then over me, and through the wall.

Immediately lightning struck right outside my window, and the loudest clap of thunder I'd ever heard violently shook the house. I had been so shaken by both events that it took me a few minutes to notice that there was no more lightning or rain, and there did not seem to be a storm around. To my surprise, the next morning when I asked others in the house if they had heard it, no one had. In the morning there was evidence that the tree right outside my window had been struck by lightning, but why had no one else even heard it? Why had there been no storm?

I was thinking about it all when it occurred to me that it might have been the rapture! Then I got really worried, thinking

The Lord had taken one look at me and decided not to take me. I started calling my Christian friends, and to my relief they were still here.

Gradually I began to feel His peace again. I knew there was something special about why He appeared to me, and I remembered the love I had seen in His eyes. I knew it was for me. I felt so unworthy because of my failings, but I started to accept that He loved me anyway, and cared enough for what I was going through that He would appear to me like that.

The demons never returned again after that night. I think it was by seeing His perfect love that it gradually cast out my fear, and I know now that demons are attracted to fear. That fear of rejection by God had been the inroad the demons had used to return and harass me.

After this experience I knew I had to move out of the party house. I would miss my friends, but after The Lord had appeared to me the grace was lifted for me to stay there. I also knew I needed to get further away from Mary, as we were too much of a temptation to each other. I decided to visit Richmond to share what had happened to me with my friends there.

I attribute my success to this: I never gave or took any excuse. *–Florence Nightingale*

Chapter 14
A Peculiar People

People were attracted to the early church. Who wouldn't be fascinated by a group that shared possessions, rejoiced nonstop, had peace beyond comprehension, and immeasurable power, never complained, and always gave thanks…? Some people joined them, others hated them, but few could ignore them. They wouldn't allow people to ignore them as they went out fearlessly sharing the gospel. This is our heritage. This is our DNA. We must stop creating safe places for people to hide and start developing fearless warriors to send out. *–Francis Chan*

Christians were called "a peculiar people" in Scripture. They were unique, and they stood out strikingly from all other people. That's why those who care too much about what others think of them do not last long in the faith, though they may resort to some more acceptable form of religion. I was already starting to see this with some of the people we led to The Lord, and was learning a lot about how faith and religion can be entirely different things.

Even so, I loved the whole spiritual scene in Raleigh, and would have loved to stay there, but I felt a drawing back to Richmond. I contacted Bart Peacher and he asked me to come for a visit. When I got there I shared what had happened to me. He politely listened, and then asked me to go to a party with him. I wanted to, but knew the temptations that would be there, and told him I needed to stay back and study. He was shocked that I would resist such an opportunity, but went on alone.

Bart came home early. I was still up reading my Bible. This was really baffling to him, and he asked me about it. This led to a conversation that I felt the presence of The Lord in. It concluded with Bart asking me to pray for him to receive The Lord. The Lord came upon him in a powerful way, and Bart was born again and baptized in The Spirit. He was ecstatic, and so was I. I also knew that I needed to move there as soon as I could to help him get established in the faith and to resist the inevitable temptations.

My Favorite Miracle

Don't postpone joy until you've learned all your lessons. Joy is your lesson. *–Alan Cohen*

I returned to Raleigh to tie up loose ends before moving back to Richmond. I decided that while I was there I would visit my mother to share with her how I had come to know that Jesus is The Lord. It was Christmas Eve, so I reasoned that with the help of "the Christmas spirit" she might be open to actually listen to me. I know now that was foolish, but I didn't know it then. The Lord did not seem to care about my immaturity because I was immature in Him.

When I came in to see her, she began raging and spewing poison about virtually everyone as usual. She did not seem coherent, and I was not even sure if she recognized me. After about a half hour of this I was not even sure if she knew I was there. Exasperated, I prayed for The Lord to bind whatever it was that had possessed her. Instantly she stopped raging, and turned and looked at me as a remarkable peace settled in the room. I was so shocked I could hardly talk.

Then she said to me, "Richard! Something has happened to you. Will you tell me about it?"

It was a voice I don't think I had heard before, and I think this may have been the first time I had actually heard my mother's voice instead of the demons. It was so amazing that it took me a bit to get going, and then I downloaded my testimony as fast as I could not knowing how long this would last.

After a few minutes Mom spoke again, saying how wonderful it was for The Lord to have done this for me. Then she asked if I thought He would do that for her. I said "yes," but before I could lead her in "the sinner's prayer," she took off with her own confessions of sin, begging for His mercy and salvation.

As I just sat and watched, The Holy Spirit came upon her, and she immediately started worshipping in a new language. I had not even said anything about tongues yet. She was now so enraptured with God that I was not sure she realized I was still there. When I got up to leave, and told her I'd come see her again the next day, I'm not sure she heard me or even noticed me leaving.

I went and shared with my Dad and younger brother and sister that Mom had received The Lord, and she was now in her right mind. This seemed too much for them to believe, but Doug and Debbie agreed to go with me to see her the next day since it was Christmas. When we saw her, she was not only in her right mind, but had been transformed from the most bitter, fearful person I have to this day ever known, to the most peaceful, loving, and kind person imaginable.

I still don't think I have ever witnessed a greater example of what it means to be born again and transformed. This undeniable miracle had a huge impact on the whole family. I got Mom a Bible and some of the great books I'd discovered that I thought would help get her off to a good start following The Lord. I also got some of the believers in Raleigh to agree to meet with her at least once a week and to take her to church with them. I then packed up and moved to Richmond.

Foundations

The person who says it cannot be done should not interrupt the person who is doing it. *–Chinese Proverb*

When I got back to Richmond, Bart was as hungry to know God as I had been. I downloaded on Bart all that I had been learning over the last few months, especially the part about The Lord restoring to His church all of the power and glory it had in the first century. Bart and I then went in pursuit of the on-fire saints in Richmond to connect with.

We soon met a man named Dudley who was as hungry for God as we were. He was a commercial artist, and had a beautiful and large apartment that he invited Bart and me to share with him, so we moved in.

Dudley had been a lifelong Church of Christ member, but had been recently baptized in The Holy Spirit, and a great passion to know The Lord had come upon him. When he tried to share this with his church elders, it did not go well. So he, Bart, and I started searching for other on-fire Christians that wanted to live The Book of Acts again. We did not have to look long to find them. So we began an amazing journey with some amazing people of God.

I was still convinced by Col. Carty's teachings and my own experience that the main place we should look were the house churches. To my surprise, there were not nearly as many of these in Richmond as in Raleigh, but we were directed to one in the west end at Sid and Delores Ryder's house.

The first meetings we attended were kind of typical of the house churches. All of the people there were serious God seekers. After a time of singing choruses, the meetings were open for anyone to share, and many did. The quality of almost everything shared was amazing. Some would share testimonies, and some a short teaching maybe five minutes in duration, but each one had uncommon depth and insight. Afterward people would mill around talking. It was hard to leave.

It was at a house church meeting at the Ryders that a young man in his early twenties shared a brief teaching about the difference between The Tree of the Knowledge of Good and Evil and The Tree of Life. His insight was profound, and the revelation so captivated me that I resolved to study this subject further. He had only spoken for about five minutes, but it resulted in me studying this subject for ten years. His five-minute message was the seed for my first book, *There Were Two Trees in the Garden*.

This book became an international bestseller, and remains a strong distributor to this day. Many consider it the most important book I have written. I regret that I do not remember this young man's name to acknowledge him. Every time I saw him in those times he seemed to have some deep and remarkable insight into the Scriptures. Besides coming to the Ryder's home group, he attended another house group led by Stephen Kaung, which I decided to visit.

Stephen Kaung had been an associate of Watchman Nee in China, and wrote most of the English books by Watchman Nee from notes he had taken from Nee's messages. Stephen wrote a number of great books under his own name, but at this time I had just discovered the Watchman Nee books. I was so looking forward to hearing Brother Kaung, I was surprised that there were only about twenty people in the meeting. However, this allowed me to spend some time with him.

Stephen Kaung was a remarkably gracious person, and had the demeanor of a wise old prophet. I loved his teaching, but even more spending the personal time with him. I returned to this group as often as I could. I was also captivated by the same gracious and peaceful feeling everyone in the small group seemed to have. They were serious God lovers and devoted biblical scholars. They had that kind of depth.

So, this group was very stabilizing for me at a time when I needed it. I think I read every single Watchman Nee book within the year, as well as Stephen Kaung's. When reading the three-volume set titled *The Spiritual Man*, I hit some parts in it that I had trouble accepting. Most of these had to do with the power of the human soul, which was also the subject of his book, *The Latent Power of the Soul*. I was disturbed that this teaching attributed the power to do miracles to the human soul, inferring that it was a counterfeit of the power of God. This was also the first thing I had read by him that I did not think was linked to Scripture, but was just flawed human reasoning.

I shared my thoughts with some mature Christians I had come to know well, and they agreed with me, saying that though they had a very high regard for the Watchman Nee books in general, there was some "serious death" in *The Spiritual Man* volumes. They did not have time to share much more than that with me, but it provoked me to go to Stephen Kaung with my concerns.

Stephen gave me the most polished, good-mannered, brush off I had ever received. He ended it by basically telling me that when I was mature enough I could understand these things.

I remember looking around the room at the others who had listened to the conversation, and all seemed to have the same "when you're as mature as we are you'll understand" look on their faces. I was immature, rough, and very clumsy spiritually and socially, but I smelled a rat! It was deception. I felt that I could see it in the room, and it was spiritual pride.

I left the Kaung house on friendly terms, but was very disturbed. I'm sure it was a trial for Stephen to be addressed on something like this from such a novice, and I wondered how arrogant I was to do this, but I believed what I said and did not compromise.

I took this to one of the elders at the Ryder house church and he very wisely said that we all have to learn to eat the meat but spit the bones out with such teachings. He reinforced how important the Watchman Nee works were and Stephen Kaung's, but felt that there was a teaching sown in some of them that would stifle faith in the gifts of The Spirit and the present operation of the power of God.

This was an important lesson for me to learn that would have a major impact on my life. It enabled me to learn from many that I would have otherwise cut off when they said things I disagreed with. Some had beliefs and teachings I seriously disagreed with, and still do. I was nevertheless able to glean very important knowledge and revelation. This also enabled me to later form genuine and mutually respectful relationships with people I differed with, and I have benefitted greatly from this. Actually, I think some of the most important things I learned came from people I had basic disagreements with about some things.

It was about this time that I first heard the Moravian Motto: "On the basics we must agree. On the other matters there must be liberty, and in all things there must be charity." I believed this to be right, and embraced it with a resolve to live it. Now I would not know how to measure the difference this made in my life and understanding, but it has been substantial.

Stephen Kaung and their "little flock" helped me to get established on some very important biblical foundations, as did the Watchman Nee books. I would recommend them to anyone today, with the explanation that there are some teachings in them that could bring confusion and doubt about the present workings of The Holy Spirit. You'll know it when you hit those, skip them and keep going.

At this time in my spiritual journey, I had already witnessed and experienced most of the gifts of The Spirit and seen the power of God in signs and wonders. I don't think I could have disbelieved in these or rationalized them away as some form of human soul power if I had even wanted to. I loved the supernatural workings of The Spirit, and I think they bring the sense of the living, ever present God with us like nothing else. After nearly fifty years of walking with God, I have not changed my opinion on this.

Stick with it. It's not that I'm so smart, but I stay with the problems longer. –*Albert Einstein*

Chapter 15
Like A Mighty Wind

One does not discover new lands without consenting to lose sight of the shore for a very long time. –*Andre Gide*

Like A Mighty Wind was the famous book written by Mel Tari about one of the most spectacular revivals of all-time in Indonesia. I still hear from Mel about once a month as he constantly circles the earth preaching, teaching, and seeking to fan the flames of revival. He is one of the burning ones whose flame never seems to dim.

Dudley, Bart, and I continued to be God hounds during this time. We would go anywhere that we thought we could find God doing something. I got a job in construction, but all I could think of all day was what meeting I could go to that night to learn or experience something of God. That's all we talked and thought about. When we did not have a meeting or service of some type to go to, we would sit around sharing with each other what we'd been learning in The Bible or from books we were reading.

This would likely sound like a crazy, boring life to one who has not experienced The Lord, but by this time I had seen quite a bit of the world and done many of the exciting things the world has to offer—nothing could even begin to compare with the excitement of getting to know The Lord. The true Christian life is the greatest and most exciting adventure that can be lived on this earth, but there is nothing on earth as boring as religion. They are not the same.

A major reason why the adventure of the Christian life cannot be compared to anything else is that it is bigger than anything else on this earth. It is an entrance into the infinite realm of the Spirit. In Scripture this earth is called a "shadow" of the spiritual, and when you begin to experience the spiritual you start to understand that it has so much more substance to it than the natural realm that comparing the substance of your shadow to you is what it is like. If we stay on the path of life, we will be in constant awe and wonder.

Dudley, Bart, and I were not just having a good exciting time—we were constantly in awe of the great things God was doing and by the previously unimaginable things we were learning and experiencing. We would visit any church or meeting where there was a visiting teacher or preacher that was recommended. In one of these we met Victor Torres. Victor was an associate of David and Don Wilkerson, founders of Teen Challenge.

Victor had been a gang leader and heroin addict who had been radically saved and delivered. After a time of getting established as a disciple under Teen Challenge, he left New York to start a new ministry in Richmond called New Life for Youth.

Victor's ministry was based in an old but large house in the inner city of Richmond. This was one of those places where it just seemed that The Lord liked to hang out. There is hardly any miracle like watching lives transformed, and this is where that was constantly happening. The worst addicts, prostitutes, or burned out hippies were being born again and having their lives transformed. Bart, Dudley, and I started visiting it as often as we could to help with the ministry, but we also received a lot ourselves from Victor and Carmen's remarkable devotion to The Lord and helping people in need.

Victor's ministry grew to become New Life Outreach International, helping tens of thousands to get free of addictions and leave the gang lifestyle. Victor's life story, *Son of Evil Street*, remains a popular book and has also been used to set many free over the years. It became a movie in 2017.

It is great to see all that The Lord has done through Victor and Carmen, but at the time we met it was an almost daily struggle for them just to keep the ministry going. It seemed that they were always short on just about everything but faith. They had to see almost daily miracles of provision to survive, and they got them. That was the great part that laid the foundation for so much future success—they had to depend on The Lord and miracles, and He will never fail those who trust in Him. Their faith grew, and so did the ministry.

Victor also introduced us to the ministries of David and Don Wilkerson, and later, Nicky Cruz. With all of the hippies being converted through the Jesus Movement, these ministries were critical for helping new believers get delivered, healed, and start their spiritual lives with sound biblical discipleship. Their resolute devotion to helping every believer walk in a manner worthy of The Lord and their calling as His people had a far-reaching impact on much of the church at the time as they became known around the world.

To a great evangelist there is nothing but evangelism. I've been blessed to know some of the greatest in our time and perhaps of all-time. I am always impacted by how they need to see people come to salvation more than they need food or water. I've been blessed to lead people to The Lord over the years, and I attribute much of this to what I received from Victor and those in his ministry. What I also got from them was a vision of how it is not enough to just lead people to Jesus, but we must help them become disciples. Like Teen Challenge, New Life was resolved to see new converts get established and stay on the straight and narrow path.

During this time, I had a dream in which my mother was standing in a dark kitchen talking to demons. When I woke up, I called the people in Raleigh who had said they would take care of her. They were embarrassed to say that they had forgotten about her. When I was able to return to see her, the fears and anger had gotten their grip on her again. She was not nearly as bad as she was before she was baptized in The Spirit, but she was definitely falling back into the darkness.

I tried to get her some spiritual help, and my brother and sister were trying to help her, but I felt then that I would probably have to move back to Raleigh for a time. I was having such a great time in Richmond that I really did not want to leave and resisted for about a year. It was truly a year of wonders, and a crucial one for preparing me for what was to come. My path would lead me back to Raleigh for a time, but first I had to experience a school of the prophets and receive the revelations of a lifetime.

A Consuming Fire

The problem is not to find the answer; it's to face the answer. –*Terence McKenna*

The early church burst into the world like an atom bomb. When the first atom bomb exploded it began a new age in which the world would live under the constant threat of destruction. When the church was born a new age was likewise begun, one in which the whole world had the door opened to eternal life, and the world would ultimately be restored to its original harmony and peace.

The early Christians defied everything that was known about human behavior. They were selfless instead of selfish. By their faith, cripples walked and lepers were healed. There were no needy or sick among them. They had an unshakable peace and joy that could not be quenched. Persecution could not stop them, death did not scare them, and the world just did not know what to do with them. Like the bomb has been the threat of destruction, the message the church has been given is a hope greater than any utopian philosophy or any other religion.

Radical Christianity as it is intended to be lived is the most revolutionary force the world has ever seen. In the first century the nations shuddered at such an unconquerable people, and they will do so again. In the first century the officials of the most powerful empire in the world cried out in dismay when just two of them limped into their city. This power and life in the early church was not an aberration, or meant to be a one-time demonstration of what The Lord could do through His people. It was meant to be a template for church life under the New Covenant.

Throughout this age, there have been sojourners who yearned to see this life again, and many have experienced it in some measure. Before the end of this age we are promised to see it in its fullness. Who would not want to be a part of this?

True faith in The Bible is not just believing that the things that happened in it were true, but it is the faith to see those things happen in our own life. Even though the life and vibrancy we experienced in the house churches was far beyond what we found anywhere else, there seemed to be a remnant within this remnant that wanted more, and some of them were after much more.

Everywhere we went exploring we seemed to find those who shared this hope. Sometimes we would walk together for a while with these new friends, and sometimes in our brief encounters we would seem to each give each other something that added to our vision.

That was the vision and hope that I was given as a new believer, and from time to time we experienced it enough to keep the fires in our hearts burning. We saw miracles. We witnessed a prophetic anointing at times that would empower words to radically change people, and sometimes even churches and organizations. We experienced God's miraculous provision for His work.

One brother even got in a ticket line for a flight to a place he believed God had called him to without any money in his pockets. He was so sure he had heard The Lord's call to a certain country that he said he knew God would supply the money somehow before he got to the counter. Without telling another soul what he needed, he had all he needed before he got to the ticket counter.

I have sat down with people to eat dinner who had no food in the house and no money to buy any. They set the table, we sat down, and gave thanks for the meal anyway. Before the prayer was finished, a knock came at the door. A woman had heard from The Lord to make this incredible feast and bring it to that house.

I was at another dinner with a few people when a large crowd showed up from another country. There was not even close to enough food to feed all of those people, but the host heard The Lord say to just start serving. Everyone ate to their fill, and there was plenty left over. Testimonies like this were very common then, and will be again.

I would not know where to start with the accounts of all of the healing miracles and dramatic demonic deliverances. There were power confrontations with witches and warlocks that would end in them either running for their lives, or falling to their knees begging Jesus to accept them.

When a cult moved into our neighborhood, Bart and I visited one of their meetings to confirm that it was a cult. Knowing we were Christians they began their instruction that night with a systematic attack on Christianity. We refuted them, but they would not listen. So we went outside and prayed for them to be removed from our neighborhood. Within two weeks they were gone.

If we weren't witnessing God move in remarkable ways, we were hearing testimonies about it. We were brand new, and so for us this seemed normal, but it was over a year before I realized that there was actually a worldwide revival taking place, and such things seemed to be happening everywhere.

Besides the Jesus Movement sweeping through the counter-culture movements, and the Charismatic Movement sweeping through perhaps every denomination, The Full Gospel Businessman's Fellowship was gathering thousands of business types and professionals to their conferences where noteworthy miracles were common, and many thousands came to The Lord.

For the first year or so I had no idea that we were just experiencing one little part of a very huge wave of The Spirit. Even so, as we were constantly looking for any place that The Spirit might be doing something, we were never disappointed, and we encountered and experienced many great things.

Pat Robertson had just started the first Christian television channel in Portsmouth, Virginia, and so I went there to check it out. This led me to Rock Church, led by John and Anne

Jimenez. This was one of the first mega-churches I had heard of. It was truly a "Spirit-filled" church and the moving of The Spirit in the services was very powerful. I thought they were some of the most blessed people in the world to be able to experience something like that every week, and I considered moving back to Virginia Beach just to be a part of it.

It would have been great, but The Lord had another plan. I had just begun to experience the Christian world. I was constantly meeting extraordinary people who were living as if citizens of another world, and they were. Miracles were their daily bread, and they spoke oracles from God. I was in constant awe of all that God was doing in those early years, but I always knew the best was yet to come.

Life shrinks or expands in proportion to one's courage. *–Anais Nin*

Afterward

I end this part of the story when I had been a Christian for a little over a year. It is hard to describe just how wonderful that year was, but it was about to get much better. I was already having visions and dreams at this point. The supernatural was becoming more of a part of my life than the natural, and it was more exciting than I had ever dreamed it could be.

It was wonderful and terrifying at the same time, but the fear was a good fear, not the kind that has torment. It is the kind that is awe and amazement, like going from thinking the world is flat and we have a few stars in the sky, to seeing the true expanse of the universe and its billions and billions of galaxies, as well as our previous concept of the world is like a speck of dust compared to it. I wondered if eternity would be long enough to learn all that I wanted to know about it.

In the second year of my walk with God I met some of the people who would help shape my life possibly more than anyone I had known until then. Some of these would have this impact with just a few words spoken to me, but they were words breathed by God, and would set remarkable events into motion.

To tell the next part of the story adequately will require its own volume because this is not just about my life. My journey is woven into this story, but from this point on, this is about encounters with God through some of His amazing people.

They helped shape my life, but they have also been shaping this world for what is to come.

Again, the true Christian life is the most exciting and fulfilling adventure that can be lived. We and this world are being prepared for the glorious age to come. The Lord really did save His best wine for last, and the wise will drink all of it that they can.

Rick Joyner

NEW

FROM RICK JOYNER

In 2018 I had a dream of a coming second American Revolution/Civil War. In this dream I saw events that are now unfolding at a rapid pace. I saw the conclusion of our present trauma, and the triumph over the evil that has been subduing our land. I saw how this victory will be accomplished. This is what I saw.

GET YOUR COPY TODAY!

HTTPS://STORE.MORNINGSTARMINISTRIES.ORG/

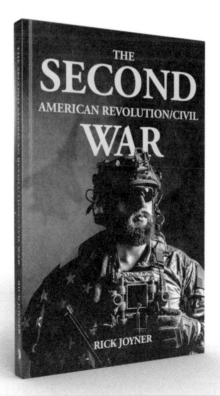

DISCOVER, SHOP, AND SAVE!

FIND ALL THE MORNINGSTAR RESOURCES YOU LOVE, PLUS NEW ITEMS ADDED ALL THE TIME!

FOR THE CURRENT CATALOG VISIT:

HTTP://MSTARM.ORG/CATALOG

TO HAVE THE CATALOG SENT DIRECTLY TO YOUR INBOX VISIT:
HTTP://MSTARM.ORG/SIGNUP

MorningStar University is for those seeking to live a high-impact life of unrelenting pursuit of the high calling to serve the King of kings with the devotion He deserves. The greatest leaders are also the greatest followers of Christ, and that is our curriculum. The true Christian life is the greatest adventure we can ever live, and it's also a life of impact like no other. If this is your resolve, MorningStar University may be for you.

WWW.MORNINGSTARUNIVERSITY.COM

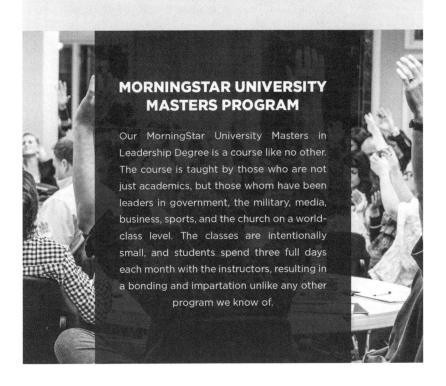

MORNINGSTAR UNIVERSITY MASTERS PROGRAM

Our MorningStar University Masters in Leadership Degree is a course like no other. The course is taught by those who are not just academics, but those whom have been leaders in government, the military, media, business, sports, and the church on a world-class level. The classes are intentionally small, and students spend three full days each month with the instructors, resulting in a bonding and impartation unlike any other program we know of.

MorningStar
Partners

Our MorningStar Partners have grown into an extraordinary global fellowship of men and women who are committed to seeing The Great Commission fulfilled in our times. Join us in equipping the body of Christ through conferences, schools, media, and publications.

We are committed to multiplying the impact of the resources entrusted to us. Your regular contribution of any amount—whether it's once a month or once a year—will make a difference!

In His Service,

PARTNER WITH US TODAY

MSTARPARTNERS.ORG
1-844-JOIN-MSP

HERITAGE INTERNATIONAL MINISTRIES CONFERENCE CENTER

Welcome to Heritage International Conference Center, a venue created to host conferences, banquets, weddings, and business meetings. We offer a 10,000 square foot ballroom with several breakout rooms, and guests enjoy walking along our indoor cobblestoned "Main Street" with lighted trees and quaint storefronts.

To learn more, please visit our website at
www.heritageconferencecenter.org

AJ Wood - Event Coordinator
ajwood@mstarm.org · 803-802-5544 ext. 223

Bridgit Vallier - General Manager
bvallier@mstarm.org

Heritage

TOWERS

Heritage Towers will be a close-knit residential community for active adult Christians. We envision attracting and mobilizing a body of believers who desire to engage in the most enjoyable, fruitful, and productive years of their lives. Heritage Towers is a major extension of MorningStar's overall mission to honor our fathers and mothers. It will be a place of discovering gifts and callings and to be equipped and deployed to fulfill all the Lord has for us.

VISIT OUR WEBSITE AT WWW.MSTARM.ORG/HC-TOWER
OR EMAIL US AT TOWER@MORNINGSTARMINISTRIES.ORG

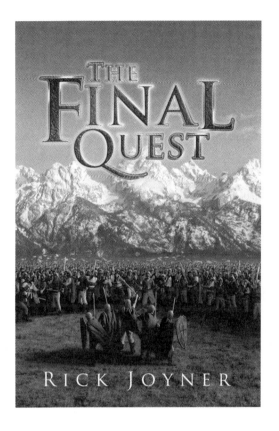

The Final Quest is a panoramic vision of the ultimate quest. It is about the greatest and last battle between light and darkness, which is happening now. Published in nearly fifty languages, it continues to call all who will go on to the greatest and most noble adventure of the age.

GET YOUR COPY TODAY!

HTTPS://STORE.MORNINGSTARMINISTRIES.ORG/

MORNINGSTAR WORSHIP

STREAMING ON

FOLLOW US

◉ MORNINGSTAR.WORSHIP

WWW.MORNINGSTARWORSHIP.COM